V.I.T.S.O.G

H.G.

WALKING

IN THE

SHADOW

OF

GREATNESS

Trusting God When You

Can't Trace Him

HOLLOWAY   GRAY

Transcribed By: Slyvia Dunnavant

Artwork By: Mtgraphix Creative Group

Published By: M. Publications LLC

Manufactured in the United States of America

DEDICATION

I am dedicating this book to my lovely wife Denise. She is the woman that God has allowed me to love and cherish for over 40 years. Through my illness, God has shown me that she is my guardian angel. I have fallen in love with her all over again.

— Holloway

"Greatness is contagious,

you will catch it if you are around it. "

-Bishop T. D. Jakes

" If you have ever wondered in your mind if God is real, can God heal or if God really knew you before the foundation of the earth?

I dare you to read Holloway's story!

After you take this journey with him, you won't question God. You will know without a doubt, He is real and He can make **all** things new!"

-*Denise Gray*
Holloway's wife

"…I met Holloway Gray personally and listening to his story and hearing the similarities in our journey made me expectant! When you read this, you will be too."

"…I quickly went from doubt and fear to hope, faith, and limitless possibility!"

Michael J. Irvin
Former Dallas Cowboy

"Great men need other great men who will help them pursue their mission.
T.D Jakes is greater because of Holloway Gray…"

"… He has exemplified excellency over the years…"

Charles E. Blake, Sr
Presiding Bishop/ C.O.G.I.C

"… Brother Gray bathes our hearts with his prayerful humility…"

"… Truly an invitation to Christian servitude…"

Bishop J. D. Ellis II
Sr. Pastor/Pentecostal Church of Christ

H.G.

FOREWORD

"Walking In The Shadow Of Greatness" reminds me of what Oprah Winfrey once told me. She said, *"It is never too late to have a turnaround."* Holloway Gray has an amazing and powerful story. His life is a reflection of resilience and triumph.

As you trace his journey, in the dust of his footprints are written the words, "comeback kid." Over the five and a half decades of his life, he has bounced back from drug addiction, diabetes, dialysis and several devastating situations.

I don't speak these words as a stranger, but as someone who has taken the same path and travelled along the same rugged road that he has. In many ways our lives are parallel; both Holloway and I experienced the devastation of dealing with drugs. I sold them, he used them, and the two of us danced down the dark side of life together. We both came out of poverty and we both lived in a world where we did the most unthinkable things, while still struggling to try and understand the call that God had on our lives.

By God's grace our footsteps were changed and our direction was turned toward our destiny. Holloway and I learned that drugs only led to a dead end road called destruction. Many people were caught up in its effects, and were not as fortunate. The simple fact that Holloway is still alive today is a testimony of God's grace and no matter what hand you are dealt in life, you can survive.

Through the pages of Holloway's story, you will get a snap shot of the world that he came from. There is crime, murder, abuse, incarceration and deception throughout his journey. By sharing his story, he will give hope to people in dark situations, who will be encouraged and strengthened to make the right choices in life. I believe his testimony will have a big impact, especially on people who have fallen into the trap of drugs and crime. However, as people read this book, it will be their passport to life, hope and living their dreams. Even though you have made mistakes, your life does not have to be a mess. Like Holloway, you too can bounce back.

-Jeff Henderson

Jeff Henderson is an award-winning executive chef, bestselling author and popular public speaker.

H.G.

TABLE OF CONTENTS

CHAPTER ONE

The Formative Years

"Parents can only give good advice or put them on the
right paths, but the final forming of a person's
character lies in their own hands."
~Anne Frank

My journey began on the backside of the mountain, in a small town called Charleston, West Virginia. I wish I could say there was something unique about the way I was raised, but there wasn't.

My parents, Mildred and Holloway Gray, Sr. were both very strict. They were typical African American parents back in the early 1960's. They were old school and didn't tolerate a lot of foolishness from us. They believed in the golden rule, and used the golden rod to rule in our house!

I have Proverbs 13:24 engraved in my bottom: "*He that spareth his rod hateth his son: but he that loveth him chasteneth him betimes.*" When it came to whippings, I was the family expert. Of all my siblings, I was the one who got them the most. Just thinking about it still sends a pain down my backside.

Although my father had four children, I was the apple of my father's eye. Without a doubt, I was the child most likely to be caught getting into some kind of mischief. My other three siblings Michael, Rena and Priscilla were smarter; they all tried to dodge trouble way more than I did.

I started my life with a very firm foundation. Due to the way my parents raised me, I always thought we were middle class. Although I didn't get everything I wanted, I never went without.

I had a meal every morning, something to wear every day and a warm place to rest my head every night. I never had to beg for food, fight for cover, or struggle to survive while I was under my parent's roof.

This may seem strange to some, but inklings of my destiny actually started in a kindergarten classroom when I was five years old. I was full of innocence and my only concern was chasing the wind.

I wasn't one of those kids who made a lot of friends; I was shyer than anything. Other children would come up and speak to me; I just didn't initiate a lot of the conversations. Even so, I still had the need to have friends and a desire to get to know people. That's about the time I met Thomas, who became my friend. I might have had two or three other friends at the time; however, it was Thomas who was my confidant. He was outgoing and very friendly, my complete opposite.

Even at our young age something just clicked with us. He really didn't seem like the average five-year-old. There was something different about him. Even though he was just a kid, his eyes were full of wisdom. If you saw him, then you saw me. When we arrived on the playground, we just gravitated towards each other.

At the end of the school year, Thomas and his family moved about thirty minutes away. He transferred to a school closer to where he lived. My family stayed in our same small community in Washington Manor, where I remained in public school until I graduated. It would be almost twenty years before I crossed paths with Thomas again.

The groundwork that was laid for me by my parents helped to keep a level of stability in my life. I had a certain time I had to be in the house. When the streetlights in our courtyard came on, I split like a cockroach. The light coming on was my magical sign the fun was over and it was time to come in out of the dark. I know a few other parents had this same rule, but some of my friends did not have to abide by this rule. Because of that, I struggled to make it home before dark.

I can still hear the other kids taunting me saying *"Don't let the dark catch you, Holloway." "Mama's boy better get in now". "It's getting late."*

Even though they hurled all those words at me, none of that mattered. I respected my parents too much not to come home. I knew if I didn't come home on time, there was going to be trouble for me and I didn't want that. Yet as a kid, I tested the waters a couple of times and decided to stay out late. My mother came out on the playground and called me by my full name, *"Holloway Gray Jr."*. After that, I realized nothing my friends had to say was worth that type of embarrassment. I came home from then on just as I was supposed to.

Although my parents were strict, I never knew abuse at home. My parents were attentive and caring; there was love all around me. Yet, none of that kept me from drifting off course.

I realize now that I was very fortunate back then. As I grew older, I began to understand there were many kids who didn't have the same story to tell. In fact, some children, who didn't live too far from me at all, ended up having very different stories and outcomes

For the most part, I grew up in a very modest home. People referred to the area I was raised in as the projects, but to me it was just a nice community.

When people think about the projects they think about bars on windows and people hanging out of doorways. Or they picture broken down, beat up buildings and random gunshots going off at night. Yet, this was not my reality at all.

Washington Manor was actually developed to help improve the decaying living conditions in our area. The complex was routinely inspected to ensure things were in good order. If there were residents who did not comply with the rules and regulations, then they would receive an eviction notice. It was as simple as that.

For me, this place was spectacular. It created a caring and concerned environment for my siblings and myself to be raised in. People watered the grass, they planted flowers and they swept the hallways. The people who lived in Washington Manor had a lot of pride for the place where they lived. After all, this was where they called home. This may sound unique when you think about the projects, but this defines the place where I grew up and this is where I developed my roots.

Everyone knew each other in our community. In fact, there was a lady in the complex we called Mrs. "J." Her house became the hangout place. She was like the "house-mother" to everybody in our area. By the end of each day, somehow we all were piled up in her home like sardines. On any given night, there were easily eight to ten people jammed up in there. This didn't really matter to Mrs. J.; she just took all of us in like we were her own children. Her son was just a few years older than I, so we all blended in like kin. Every time we were there, it was just like being at home. We would always play music and act silly. Sometimes, she would even feed us lunch and dinner.

At Mrs. J.'s house, there was a particular girl named Denise; she was always there. She was ten at the time and I was eleven. Denise stayed a couple of streets over from me. Her mother and father lived in a housing development just outside of Washington Manor. She would come into our community just to hang out. Before I knew it, her friends were my friends and my friends were hers.

Denise had two older brothers so she was sort of a tomboy, but that was perfect because she just blended in with all of us. We were like one big family; we were all close. As for Denise and I, this was the beginning of a lifelong friendship.

I must have been about nine or ten years old when I was introduced to Christ. Sunday school and church service cemented a lesson of God's redeeming love in my heart. It bolted down His word in my heart, which would make it easily accessible over my life. Even when I would forget who I was, I would always remember who God was. Just like my neighborhood and community surroundings created a physical foundation for me, this was the beginning of my spiritual foundation. This gave me a genuine respect for religion and Christianity.

Proverbs 22:6 states, "*Train up a child in the way he should go: and when he is old, he will not depart from it.*" This scripture was my corner stone. It was the anchor for my shipwrecked soul. It gave me the strength to hold on through my life's course. When I examine the twists and turns my life has taken, my introduction to Christ was the most critical and crucial thing that could have happened to me when I was growing up.

* Scripture Reference

"Be not forgetful to entertain strangers: for thereby some have entertained angels unawares."

Hebrews 13: 2 (KJV)

* Prayer

Lord, let me make an impact in some young person's life. It might be a word of encouragement, but in some way let me touch the next generation.

CHAPTER TWO

The Journey Begins

"Sometimes it's the journey that teaches you a lot about your destination."

~ Drake

By the time I was eleven years old, I began to leave behind all I knew to be true. Even though I was old enough to know right from wrong, the distractions of the world were more enticing than the path I had been taught to follow. I began to hang around kids who were a couple years older than me, and although I liked hanging out with "big boys," it ended up costing me more than I bargained for in the long run.

We were very manipulative and crafty young people. As a group, we traveled as a family. We were our own little gang, and together we had each other's backs. We protected our secret little sins and made sure our parents were not aware of the things we were getting into.

The more we hung out together, the easier it was to stumble down the road of destruction. It started with a sip of beer; then it advanced to things like cigarettes, hard liquor and marijuana. We were naïve and didn't realize the dangers of doing things we simply were not old enough to understand. I had never experienced anyone dying, so it didn't dawn on me my actions could be deadly.

In our group drinking became the norm. We weren't used to the side effects at first. It seemed like the worst ones were getting sick from drinking too fast, or drinking on an empty stomach. It wasn't long before we were able to tolerate it. After a while, we just began to equate drinking with simply having fun.

We drank everything we could put our hands on. We became so experienced with alcohol that we even learned what proof strength each drink had in it. From that point, it was easy to determine which drink would give us the quickest buzz for the least amount of money. Once we mastered drinking, it was time to move on to something else.

Alcohol was just a teaser for our tantalized taste buds; we then began to crave something stronger. Our experimentation went from cigarettes, to wine and beer to liquor. Before long we were popping pills and drinking on a regular basis every weekend.

At that age, drinking became important to us. There were times I had way too much to drink and I knew I was flat-out drunk. There had to be someone there to watch over me in the event I did anything crazy. Yet, it was still all in good fun. Throwing up, falling down, it was just a part of the thrill. It was just something we all went through. When we were drinking, we would laugh and make jokes. Someone would fall down, and someone else would pick them up. The bottom line is, we fine-tuned our drinking skills, and we did whatever it took to make things work.

This became our weekend routine. During the weekdays, we all went to school and did homework. Monday through Fridays were days for reading, writing and arithmetic. However, Saturdays and Sundays, were all about the beer, the booze and the fun. When the school week ended, we were all on the run.

When I think back on this time in my life, I realize my actions and behaviors could be summed up as being influenced simply by peer pressure. I hung with a group of kids that didn't have a lot of limitations. I didn't want to feel left out, so I joined the crowd. One thing led to another and before I knew it, I was like a car on a road covered in black ice, spinning out of control.

I think at first I was just looking for friendship. There was a part of me that wanted to connect with someone. It just happened to be that the people I connected with were right there in my community. I was comfortable with them, I felt covered by them, but I was also caught up with them. We grew up together and we got in trouble together. As we traveled down this devious road, we developed a code of ethics amongst ourselves; what we did in private was kept in private.

It might be hard to believe, but none of us came from a bad family. Unlike what the statistics may have stated, the majority of us came from two parent homes. It was rare for us to be associated with a kid who did not have a father around. In fact, in most cases, both parents were working. We all had great families and some of my friends came from Christian homes. So, we went through great efforts to make sure our parents never found out about our weekend activities.

Being young and introduced to drugs was like being a kid at the grand opening of a brand new candy store. We began to contemplate what the effects would be of the drugs. What type of experience would it make us have? Would it make us go down, or would it make us come up? Or, would it just make us act crazy?

I don't believe any of us thought we would become addicted; no one ever thought we would be strung out. It was no one's desire to become a junkie; it was just exciting hanging out together and attempting to try something new. There wasn't any rhyme or reason to what we were doing. There weren't any conscious thoughts given to the fierce consequences, side effects or long-term reactions.

We were just curious kids. We took chances and we thought we would never get caught. The entire time we experimented with drugs, our lives dangerously danced on the edge of a cliff, but no one ever thought about falling off.

We were willing to try anything and everything. There was a strong curiosity in our spirits. We were always wondering how things worked. After we experienced our first high, there was this sensation that took us over the top. From that point on, we were constantly chasing the feeling of that first hit.

Little did we know that with every drink we took and every joint we smoked, we were beginning to play a dangerous game of cat and mouse. We never caught what we were chasing, but what we were chasing was about to catch us.

* Scripture Reference

"The angel of the Lord encampeth round about them that fear Him, and delivereth them."

Psalm 34: 7 (KJV)

* Prayer

Lord, please allow me to glean from those You have placed along my path during this journey. I don't know all the relationships You have linked to my destiny, but keep me open to those people who will push me toward my purpose.

H.G.

CHAPTER THREE

Walking On The Wild Side

"Growing up is all about getting hurt and then getting over it.
You hurt. You recover. You move on. Odds are pretty good
you're just going to get hurt again, but each
time you learn something."
~Jim Butcher, White Night

Time waits for no one, and it was not waiting for me. As I got older, my experimental escapades began to escalate. I had already tried beer, liquor and wine. Now, it was time to try something new and more challenging. By the time I was fourteen years old, my friends and I began to experiment with popping pills.

It was around that time I had my first bad encounter with

drugs. An older guy who was dating my sister, Priscilla, ended up giving me some amphetamines. We referred to these pills in the streets as "white crosses." White crosses were a stimulant. They gave you a euphoric feeling and caused you to act in very abnormal ways. Some of the side effects would increase your blood pressure and cause your heart rate to go up. This was the first time I had taken this particular pill and I had no idea what to expect. The guy gave me four pills, so I just took all of them at once. Who knew this was entirely too many pills to take at once? I didn't realize what I had done; before I knew it, my heart was racing like crazy and I was experiencing heart palpitations. The changes in my body made me freak out because I had never experienced these type of symptoms. As my heart rate began to speed up, I didn't know what to do. I felt completely out of control.

I was able to get myself together enough to call the guy who had given me the pills. With my hands dripping wet with sweat, I asked him, *"What in the world did you give me?"* He paused a few minutes before he responded. Then he asked, *"How many pills did you take?"*

H.G.

I couldn't understand why he would ask me such a question. He had given me four pills; of course, I had taken all of them. When I told him how many pills I had taken, I thought he had dropped the phone. For a moment I heard nothing but silence.

Then he let me know I was only supposed to take one. According to him, my only solution was to coat my stomach. He recommended I drink some milk. It wasn't as if I could go to my parents and ask for help. So I had to take him up on his suggestion, and hope it worked.

Feeling like my heart was going to jump out of my chest, I headed to the grocery store with some of my close friends. They were accompanying me to make sure I was going to be okay. Hoping this was going to be the solution I needed, I downed an entire gallon of milk in an alley behind our complex. I slid down on the ground as I waited to get some relief. It took about three or four hours for me to finally come down. After the drug wore off and I was back to normal, I was able to get home before anyone at the house knew what had happened.

There was no doubt this was a bad experience. Though the event shook me, it was not enough to make me quit doing drugs. I continued to try to find a higher high or a lower low. I went from taking speed, to taking downers. My friends and I tried it all. We did 714s, Red Devils and whatever else we could get our hands on.

By this time, the gang I hung around with was all in high school. Now that we were older, we didn't have weekend limitations; we could now get away with doing drugs during the week. We were so carefree we even started to go to school high. Before classes, we would smoke a joint to get our day started. Sometimes we'd go as far as dropping Acid or LSD.

Taking LSD was a lot different than just doing pot. While a joint might give you a buzz for a few hours, LSD would leave you high for twelve to thirteen hours at a time. The drugs we

were taking were very strong. They could cause you to
hallucinate or do crazy things. They would make you act in all
kinds of courageous ways.

Each person's reaction to the drugs might be a little different;
it all depended on the person's body. I had some friends who
had bad experiences with Blotter Acid. Seeing somebody trip
off acid was no joke. When they finally came down from their
high, it was as if they had been in a bad fight. They were
totally exhausted. The only difference was they weren't
fighting with anyone; they were fighting with themselves.

It's amazing how all of this started out just for kicks. I will
admit it was a lot of fun, but drinking and popping pills were
and still are a very dangerous combination. After a while, it
runs havoc on your mind and your body. When I was taking it,
I began to chase something I could never catch, and run after
something I would never find. It was such a vicious cycle with
such an unpredictable ending. When you are on a road going
nowhere, you don't realize it until you come to a dead end.

As I got deeper into drugs, I also began to shop lift. There were times we would steal as a group, but many times I would just go by myself. I realized if I was by myself, I didn't have to worry about anyone telling on me. I also felt it was easier not to get caught if I was alone.

It was close to the holidays and I wanted to buy Christmas gifts for Priscilla, Rena and my mother. I knew I could easily lift some small trinkets, bracelets or jewelry items. So, with Christmas gifts on my mind, I put on a loose fitting jacket and headed to the Diamond Department store downtown. "The Diamond" was one of the premier places to buy gifts. Their slogan was "Christmas gifts galore, gifts on every floor."

The place was spectacular. It was like a winter wonderland. It had a huge window in the front of the store with nothing but toys in it. One display held a handsome model train set where you could push the button of the display and watch it ride by. I knew this store would be busy and there were bound to be plenty of distractions to keep me from being caught.

When I arrived at the store, there was so much hustle and bustle, I figured it was going to be easy to get in and out without anyone even noticing me. I already had a tentative list of the things I planned to pick up: a necklace, a charm bracelet and maybe even a ring. I just wanted something I could slip into my jacket, my pocket, or my trousers and be on my way.

I hit the ladies department like I was on a shopping spree. As I looked around the room, I lifted a couple of items and headed to the escalator. As I rode down the escalator, I glanced toward that big window. I just could not pass up the chance to press the button and make the train go around once before I left. I walked over to the display and as I hit the button, I felt a slight tap on my shoulder. It was a big tall man in a blue suit behind me. An undercover cop had been watching me from the second floor. Placing his hand on the top of my shoulder, he said, *"Come with me young man."* I couldn't believe it. My shopping spree had come to an end and I had been caught.

They took me to the security office until the police came to pick me up and take me to the police station. There was no doubt this was not going to be a good day for me.

As I rode in the back seat of the police car, my heart sank in my chest. What in the world was I going to tell my parents? I couldn't even muster up the words in my mind to make this begin to make sense to them. It wasn't just about being caught, but how this would make my dad look. This was going to be a big slap in my father's face; he worked in the warehouse of the Diamond Department Store.

This would be a double embarrassment for him. It wasn't just being caught, but being caught at the store my father worked for. What was I thinking? I knew bad news traveled fast. All I could do was pray the word did not reach him before I could get home. Although I guess it didn't matter because I was going to be in trouble no matter what.

To my surprise, the police officer did not take me to jail; they took me home instead. I held my head down as the officer knocked on my door. It was my father who answered.

The police officer asked, *"Are you Mr. Holloway Gray?"* Not having a clue of what had transpired, my father just said, *"Yes."* The police officer explained to my father what happened. Then he took out some paperwork for him to sign and released me into his custody. I wasn't sure if this was going to be any better than going to jail, especially since my father had found out I was shoplifting where he worked.

I was shocked my father wasn't upset after the police left. He really didn't do anything; he just walked away. I could not believe his response. My older sister Priscilla came out of her room. She said, *"Boy, what have you done? You are going to be the death of Mama yet!"* Normally, I wouldn't even pay any attention to what she had to say but it was different this time, there was something a little strange going on. Dad seemed extra quiet and this was a little unusual.

My mom was really the disciplinarian in our home. My father would speak to you in an even tone and still get his point across. He would scold you, but he would do it in a way that made you think about what you had done. My father's words carried weight. When he said something, it spoke volumes. Sometimes his silence was a form of communication. He used his words like a knife. He was very precise with what he had to say. Yet, this particular evening he wasn't saying anything.

Then I realized there was a void in the house. There was an unusual sense of quietness around. I realized my mother was missing. Looking around the house, I asked, "*Where is mama at?*" At first, no one said a word. Then Priscilla said, "*She is in the hospital.*"
"*What do you mean she's in the hospital,*" I asked?
"*She had a stroke today, and they took her to the hospital,*" said Priscilla as she waited to get a reaction from me.

When she said that, I fell to the floor and placed my hands over my head. "*Wow,*" was all I could say. My mind began to race back and forth like the train set in the window of the Diamond Department Store. While I was plotting to steal, my mother had a stroke. A heavy level of guilt began to cover me like a dark cloak. This was a much more severe punishment than jail or even prison. My mind raced with all the things I have done that could have contributed to this. It sickened me to think of how my actions could have caused this chain of events.

I felt God had to be punishing me for my actions by allowing this to happen to my mother. Surely, if I had not been shoplifting, she would never have had a stroke. My mind began to play tricks on me. I thought if I had never been picked up for shop lifting, my mother would not have gotten sick. I actually blamed myself for my mother's stroke. I kept thinking, if I wouldn't have been somewhere I wasn't supposed to be, she wouldn't have had a stroke.

After I pulled myself together, we went to Charleston Memorial Hospital to see my mother. I was really hoping everyone kept quiet about what I had done, at least until she got home.

The reality was, my shoplifting got overlooked. It was nothing compared to our family having to deal with my mother's recovery from a stroke. She would have a long road ahead of her until she got back to normal. Her entire left side was partially paralyzed, so she would have to go through full rehabilitation. She would have to learn how to use her left side all over again.

The start of my mother's recovery was very slow. It took months for her to get back to normal.
I watched as my mother's health progressed. This entire process was very difficult for me. I was plagued with guilt and shame. I knew while she was recovering from her stoke, she was also having to deal with the knowledge of what I had done. This only compounded the emotional guilt I was experiencing. I could never grasp this was a coincidence; I felt I was to blame.

Watching my mother struggle to get back to normal wasn't easy. I knew I needed to apologize to her. It wasn't until some years later that I was able to separate the turn of events. Finally, I realized the two things really didn't have anything to do with one another, but I knew God always has a plan. It may have been to teach me a lesson. Crime does not pay and the cost may be something more than you are willing to pay.

Once my mother recovered, she was very upset with me for my actions. I don't think it was because I stole from a place my father was employed at, but it was much deeper than that. Deep inside, she knew I was not demonstrating the character of the person she had raised me to be.

I knew she was ashamed because she had raised me much better than that. Deep inside, I knew it to be true. Yet, I didn't think I could do better. The simple fact was, I was a person who liked to take chances. Sometimes I got away with it, and sometimes I didn't. This time it was going to cost me, even more than I knew.

* Scripture Reference

"For he whom God hath sent speaketh the words of God: for God giveth not the Spirit by measure unto him. The Father loveth the Son, and hath given all things into his hand. He that believeth on the Son hath everlasting life: and he that believeth not the Son shall not see life; but the wrath of God abideth on him."

John 3:34-36 (KJV)

* Prayer

Lord, don't allow the enemy to hold me captive when it is Your desire I be free. Today, let me walk in divine freedom and divine peace. I will only believe Your report. It will be a light unto my path and lamp unto my soul.

CHAPTER FOUR

Destiny Distraction: The Death of My Dad

"My father gave me the greatest gift anyone could give another person; he believed in me."

~Jim Valvano

It was hard to believe what started as something fun was turning into something very unpleasant. Like a fluttering fly, I was being pulled into a spider web I could not get out of. By the time I was seventeen, getting high was no longer an option; it was a necessity. I began to crave drugs like a hungry man needed food.

Yet, what I didn't realize was that while I was getting high, a very valuable part of my life was slipping away from me.

At first, I didn't really pay any attention when my dad started coughing because I was too busy keeping up with the boys in the neighborhood. When he began to slow down, I would slip out into the streets to take a hit. Before long, the signs were undeniable. While I was chasing my next high, my dad had been caught by cancer.

My father had always played a very strong role in our household. Like a lot of men in West Virginia, he spent much of his early life making a living in the coal mines. Working in the damp dim conditions of the mines helped many men make a living for their families. Yet, no one realized the amount of dust that would accumulate in their lungs would make the job more costly than what it was worth.

My dad had always been my role model of what a man should be. To this day, I have his image engraved in my mind. He stood about 5'9 and weighed around two hundred pounds. No matter what was going on, he was always pleasant. In fact, I don't think he ever met a stranger. He was like a walking encyclopedia and he had this wonderful sense of wisdom. He didn't mind sharing his golden nuggets with anyone who was willing to listen.

A lot of times my friends would end up hanging around my house to engage in conversation with my father. He didn't mind making sure they got his take on whatever was going on at the time.

It was sort of funny. I would be running around doing something else while they chatted with him. Then later, one of my friends would say, "*Hey Holloway, your dad said this...or your dad said that.*" Even though they were trying to be cool, they were completely caught up in whatever my dad had to share with them.

After a while my dad's stories grew short; his lessons in life were now few and far between. He was fighting the fight of his life. In a short period of time, his two hundred pound body dwindled down to about one hundred twenty five pounds. Little to my knowledge, he had developed Black Lung Disease and the cancer had literally eaten away at him.

In the latter days of his life, just visiting him in the hospital was my ultimate challenge. It was hard to look into his sunken eyes and see his frail body and realize, here was the man who I called Dad. The man who had carried me as a boy was starting to look like a corpse and it was almost unbearable for me to watch.

There were times I avoided going to the hospital because I could not stand to see him that way. As the cancer continued to take a toll on him, I literally had to force myself to go to the hospital. When I did, I felt he was only a shadow image resting in the hospital bed; it was not my father anymore. He was a person eaten up by cancer.

On November 13, 1974, the day my family had been dreading finally happened. My father lost his fight to cancer. I now had to face some hard facts; as much as I wanted to keep him with me, my father was gone. At the age of seventeen, I had to deal with the fact I had to grow up.

After my father died, everything he told me came back to my remembrance. I reflected on all the things he taught me over the years. It was hard to face the truth; I had just lost one of the most important people in my life.

Once I knew he would no longer be around, I realized how much I cherished him. When he died, I realized I didn't really appreciate him as much as I should have. Yet, my memories of him were all very fond. His memories got me through the roughest times of my life.

There is no doubt that losing my father at the age of seventeen had a tremendous effect on my life. I was just coming to grips with who I was becoming and the person who was designed to help me transition into adulthood was gone. I had to figure out who to lean on when I no longer had my rock.

Over time, I tried to understand how my father could be taken away from us so quickly, but I couldn't. My siblings Michael, Priscilla and Rena couldn't grasp it either. Therefore, we didn't talk about it. We just tried to handle it in on our own way. There wasn't an easy way to put it; we just managed.

The one thing we realized, with our father now being gone: we had to focus on mama. It was evident that just as we had leaned on dad, so did she. For the life of me, I didn't know how she was going to make it. There were four of us who still needed her. Although I knew she had to be in a lot of pain herself, she never let us see her cry.

The majority of my life my mother had been a case-worker for the Department of Welfare. She had worked with all kinds of people in various situations. Consequently, when she had a situation of her own, she just dealt with it and moved on. Her biggest battle wasn't adjusting; it was fighting with the Coal Mine organization to get what was rightfully due to our family.

Working in the coal mines for almost three decades had cost my father his life. However, getting compensation took my mother several years of red tape and litigation. In the end, the doctor's report revealed what we all knew. He died from black lung disease. After almost five years, she was able to get a lump sum settlement and his pension for the rest of her life.

Losing my dad was more than just a void in my life; there was also a shift that took place in my spirit. My safe haven was gone. Without him, there was no one to protect me from the things life held ahead. From that point on, my life took a turn in a more destructive direction. As I tried to fill the new void in my life, I continued to dance down a dangerous road.

The first thing that caught me off guard was my friend, Tiny; he got caught in a very bad situation. Tiny, used to be a part of our group in the community. One day he was trying to get some quick money. He decided to go down to the corner store and hold them up.

On the corner of Capital Street there was a small store called Boraski's and Sons. It was small, but they did pretty good business in the community. They had been there for a long time and had a well-established clientele. Sometimes Old Man Boraski (that's what we called the owner) was in the store by himself. I guess Tiny thought catching Mr. Boraski alone would be a good opportunity to grab some cash and run.

At the time, I didn't know what he was thinking about, and why did he take a pistol with him? I am not sure if he was nervous or anxious, but somehow he ended up shooting and killing Mr. Boraski. Mr. Boraski was a pillar in our community. He was well-liked and well respected.

Mr. Boraski's death was devastating to the community. When I found out about this, I was in total shock. Tiny had grown up on the outskirts of the projects. He would always come and play with us. We had been friends for years. I had known him since I was seven years old. Now, ten years later he'd made a mistake that changed his life.

The community was in such an uproar about Mr. Boraski's death, they decided to make an example out of Tiny. They held him over in the Juvenile System until his eighteenth birthday so he could be tried as an adult. They sentenced him: ten-years to life. To my knowledge, he was released once for a brief period of time, but then he returned for a parole violation.

Tiny was just one clear example for me that life is all about choices. The wrong choice could change your direction for a lifetime. As I was coming to grips with Tiny's choice; I had to make a choice of my own.

Over the years my friendship with Denise had grown. From the time we were about fifteen years old, people viewed us as an item. I don't think we said anything official, but everyone around us considered us to be boyfriend and girlfriend.

There was something about her that had my attention. Not only was she attractive, but she also had a good personality. She was also very independent and she wasn't afraid to speak her mind. Even at an early age, she stood out amongst the other girls. Some of her girlfriends were also friends of mine, but there was something different about Denise.

Time was very favorable to Denise. She transformed from a tomboy who hung out with us guys, to a beautiful young lady. Right before my eyes, she blossomed like a flower in the spring.

The year after my dad died, Denise was a junior in high school and I was a senior. We were so close we even shared a locker at school together. One day Denise came up behind me at school and said, *"Holloway, I have to tell you something."*
I don't know why I didn't ask her to wait, but I insisted she tell me when we got to the locker.
Before I knew it, she blurted out, *"I am pregnant."*

I took one look at her face and I knew I was not about to give her the answer she wanted. All I could manage to roll off my tongue was, *"Are you sure?"* She still seemed perky when she responded back to me with, *"Yes."*

I grabbed my head and pushed my body into the locker and said, *"You know this just can't be. There is no way you can have this baby. I am not ready to be a father."* I was in complete panic mode.

I didn't want to believe her. I was frantic more than anything. I think the reason I was so afraid was I couldn't imagine going home and telling my mother my girlfriend was pregnant. For the life of me, I could not picture myself doing that.

Denise and I continued to talk briefly. I knew I sounded like a broken record. All I could say was, *"No, you can't have this baby. You just can't do it."* Her response was simple. She said, *"But I have to."* We could not agree about what to do, so I told her *"You just get your stuff and get out of my locker."* I knew it sounded childish, but my back was up against the wall and I didn't know what to do.

Before I knew it, she walked away without saying good-bye. My mind began to race like never before. I could barely take care of myself, how in the world was I going to take care of this baby? Having a child was just not in my plans. I couldn't comprehend why she just didn't see that. It never once dawned on me Denise had not planned to have a child either. I could only think about myself. The next day it was final; we broke up.

I really didn't have a reason; I guess I was just mean. Denise was a strong young lady. She didn't buckle, nor did she budge. Even though I knew she was upset, she didn't allow my decision to change her mind about having the baby. Committed to dealing with the consequences of our actions, she went to her mother, Mrs. Mary Morgan. Her mother chose to stand by her side.

To this day, I have to thank God for Denise's mother. She was a praying woman. She did not let my decision have any impact on their life. She clearly let me know Denise was going to keep the baby and they would get through it with or without me.

The following year when Denise gave birth to our son Jody, I had already left the state. I got into some trouble with the law. One of my friends and I wanted to make some quick money so we were selling fake pot. We ended up selling our fake pot to some undercover policemen. This was not like shoplifting from Diamond's Department Store. This was a felony, and I stood a good chance of doing some serious time.

The judge that I appeared before was known for giving stiff sentences to African Americans. As I prepared to throw myself upon the mercy of the court, I felt like my luck was running out. I had a few minor offenses already, but up until this time, I didn't have anything this severe on my record. The day I went before the judge, he took one look at me and said, *"If you come before me again, the only thing you will need is your tooth brush."*

I knew he meant there wouldn't be any more leniencies. If I messed up again, I was going to prison. I knew me. There was no doubt I was going to mess up again. I knew I needed to come up with another plan. I didn't have a lot of options, so I decided to go to school out of state. I chose to go to school in Columbus, Ohio.

Although I loved Denise, I was in no way ready to face dealing with a family. Therefore, I chose to do the only logical thing in my mind - to run. I was running from a dilemma. I was running from a devastating situation. Yet, I could not run from my destiny.

* Scripture Reference

"Honor your father and mother, which is the first commandment with promise:"

Ephesians 6:2 (KJV)

Our parents are placed in our lives for a strategic purpose. There is a divine role for our parents to help us transition from childhood to adulthood. If for whatever reason they are not there to assist us with the transition, there is something missing in our lives.

* Prayer

Lord, I will honor my parents because I know You placed me in their lives for a purpose. They have helped guide and develop me for a reason. Let me love them and celebrate them for as long as You have them in my life.

CHAPTER FIVE

Back Tracking: Time To Go Home

"There is no place like home."

~L. Frank Baum,

(From the book, "The Wonderful Wizard of Oz")

Once Denise and I broke up, I didn't look back. I just left. I decided it was time to make a fresh start. I packed my clothes and moved to Columbus, Ohio. Determined to do something different, I attended the Ohio Institute of Technology. I'm not even sure why I chose technology because I had not studied it in high school. I guess I just thought technical school was a way for me to get away from West Virginia and get out of the situation I was in. I wanted to take a chance at something that did not resemble what I had done before.

The first year I was in Ohio was smooth sailing. I made good grades and even made the Dean's List. In fact, things were so good; I called a good friend of mine to join me. We had been in school together most of our lives. I was sure he would have liked this opportunity as well. We were always close and I considered him to be one of my closer friends from the community.

Looking back on the decision to call him reminds me of the story in the Bible about Abraham's nephew and family coming out of Sodom. Upon the deliverance of Lot's family, they were instructed not to turn around and look back at the destruction of Sodom and Gomorrah under any circumstances. Lot's wife was not obedient, and turned around and looked back. She was instantly turned into a pillar of salt. I realize now the reason Lot's wife was turned into a pillar of salt was because she could not leave her past. She was so hung up on what was behind her, she couldn't move into her destiny. Similarly, once my friend arrived in Ohio, things began to change. We started partying, hanging out, doing drugs and getting into our old dirt. I lost my focus on school and things got a lot harder. In no time at all, my grades took a nosedive. I went from A's and B's to just trying to pass my classes.

After about a year my friend said, *"I don't think this is going to work for me."* Disheartened with his attempt to make it in college, he headed back to Charleston.

Even without him there, I tried to hold on for a while longer. Yet, after another three or four months I realized I was not cut out for college. I couldn't concentrate, keep up or contemplate what I was supposed to do next. The bottom line was that I didn't give school my full attention. I had to admit, it was time to go home. I called my mom and said," *I'm coming back home."*

When I got back home, it was evident I had plenty of unfinished business. The first thing I had to do was to address Denise. She had given birth to my son Jody while I was gone. I had not seen him or her in about a year and a half. Jody was now fifteen months old. This was something I knew I had to resolve.

As soon as my feet settled on Charleston soil, I had to swallow my pride. Now that I was back in West Virginia, I began to feel guilty. My father had always told me, *"If you are going to do something, make it count."* I made my way to Denise's house. I could not believe how foolish I had been.

I had to begin to work on making things count in my life. I had no idea what I was going to say when I saw her. I didn't even know if she would open the door. I just knew I had to at least go.

As I stood outside Mrs. Morgan's front door, the palms of my hands began to sweat. I didn't know what to expect. When her mother opened the door, my heart began to jump.
"Hello, Mrs. Morgan, is Denise here?" I blurted out.
She looked at me with her warm inviting eyes and said, *"Yes, give me a moment. I will go get her for you."*

I sat on the couch just waiting for Denise to come out. Everything in me was on edge. I knew I had been wrong for staying away so long. My biggest question was: how in the world do I make this right now?

With all the grace Denise always carried, she came out to greet me. She looked so good. Just her presence was like a breath of fresh air to me. Once she smiled at me, all the things I was dealing with started to melt away.

Before I could even say hello, I asked, *"Can I see Jody?"*
"You are not going to say, how have you been doing? What's been going on?" she asked with a smile on her face.
We both started to laugh a little. Our laughter took the edge off a very awkward situation. Then she went and got my son and placed him in my arms. The warmth of his body connected with my heart. For a moment, time stood still. I could see my likeness in his face. When I looked at him, it was as if I was looking at my reflection in a mirror. I knew I was looking at a part of me.

As I held him, I began to think about how my father had raised me. I was overcome with guilt. How selfish could I be?

What on earth was I thinking? I knew coming back home was my only option. Seeing my son for the first time started to open my eyes.

I had been gone far too long. My dad's words began to echo in my ears and I knew I had to make my life count. It was time to start by making things count with my son.

I looked at Denise and I looked at Jody. I knew I had two of the most valuable people I could ask for right before me. Trying to hold back the tears, I asked Denise, *"Can you let me back in your life?"*
Her response did not come right away, but she finally said, *"Yes, Holloway, but only if you are serious."*

Her answer warmed my heart. I knew I didn't want someone else to raise my son. I wanted to be there for him. I wanted to be in his life. I knew I was responsible for him being in the world, and I wanted to be the one who made a difference in his life.

Without a doubt, getting back with Denise was a step in the right direction for me. I began to thank God for her allowing me back into her life. She was definitely a good woman, and I needed her to help me develop some form of stability in my life.

Once Denise said yes, we began to try and make the best of things. We found a place and moved in together. I got a couple of part time jobs and started working so I could help take care of her and Jody. Denise was always very independent. She already had a good paying job working at a telephone company.

By the time Jody was about five years old, I realized I couldn't keep taking Denise for granted. She was a good woman who was caring and had a great personality. I had already lost her once and I didn't want to chance losing her again. If I needed somebody to keep me grounded and rooted, she was that woman.

* Getting Married *

Five years after Jody's birth, I asked Denise to marry me. Getting married just seemed to make sense. Jody was about to start kindergarten and he still had Denise's last name. I wanted him to have my name; after all he was my son. In fact, I wanted both of them to have my last name.

I began to reflect on how I was raised. I had both of my parents. I wanted my son to have the same thing. I didn't want him to be considered a bastard child with no father present in the home. I hadn't known many kids like that when I was growing up.

I was about twenty-three years old when I married Denise. Most of my friends thought I was crazy for getting married at such an early age, but they didn't realize I wasn't about to give up on what I had in Denise. She was my friend, she was my comrade, and I wanted her to be my wife.

Since my father's passing away, the next closest man in my life was my mother's father. He was somewhat crippled and had a very difficult time getting around. I knew he might have a problem getting to the wedding, but it was very important for me to have him there. I decided to ask him if we could have the wedding in his home.

Without any hesitation, he responded with a big, *"Yes."* I was so happy. He had played such a major part in my life growing up that I wanted him to be a part of our union. My grandfather's response was just a confirmation that all flags were flying in our direction.

Now that we were getting married, I was still fighting the words of a lot of my friends. Getting married at twenty-three was not a good idea to them. They made comments like *"You are too young, and you got a lot going for you. Wait until you get other women out of your system."* However, deep in my heart I knew I was making the right decision. I had a good woman, and I was stepping up to the plate to seal the deal with her.

My former pastor agreed to perform the ceremony at my grandfather's house. The day Denise and I got married was a picture perfect day. Our wedding was a small intimate gathering of family and friends. I had my best man, Larry, and Denise had her matron of honor, Joyce. We probably had about thirty-five friends and family members in attendance to celebrate our blissful occasion.

Three hours after our quiet union, Denise and I had a ball at our reception. We had family, friends, food and fun at the King Center. Over a hundred people turned out. They helped us rock the night away as we stepped into our journey as man and wife.

This seemed like the perfect setting for a wonderful journey, but no one could have imagined how rocky this road was about to be for both of us. To everyone's surprise, I had slipped out between the wedding and the reception to get a fix. I was able to separate myself just long enough from my new bride to get what I needed to make me straight. I got a shot of cocaine to help keep me rolling along until the end of the night.

I laughed and I socialized with everyone. I was the life of the party. Little did anyone realize that I had a drug addiction, which dragged me along like a puppet on a string. I was joining my life to Denise, but I was already married to cocaine. This is how our life together would begin.

* Scripture Reference

"But when he came to himself, he said, 'How many of my father's hired servants have bread enough and to spare, and I perish with hunger! [18] *I will arise and go to my father, and will say to him, "Father, I have sinned against heaven and before you,* [19] *and I am no longer worthy to be called your son. Make me like one of your hired servants."'*

Luke 15: 17-19

* Prayer

Lord, like the prodigal son I have drifted away, but I am ready to come home. I realize that I am Your child, and I have an inheritance that has been stored up just for me. Let nothing I have done keep me away from the riches You have purposed for my life. I openly run into Your caring and compassionate arms. I am coming home.

CHAPTER SIX

Two Become One

"Marriage is more than sharing a life together, it's building a life together. What you do now is for both, and what is said now is for both. Now your purpose is for the Kingdom and giving glory to the image of God."
~Norm Wright

When Denise and I got married, it was the beginning of a new chapter in my life. After we were married our lives were full of so much joy and excitement. Although we lived together before, it was different now that we were officially married. I was ready for whatever life had to offer and so was she. It was nice in the beginning. I didn't understand why I waited so long to take the plunge; there was no doubt that she was a good woman. Bottom line, she was the woman that I needed in my life.

It was hard at first financially. I struggled trying to make ends meet and help take care of my new family. Without a college education or hands-on experience, it was difficult to find a decent job in West Virginia. Since I couldn't get one good full-time job, I worked two part-time jobs. I would work from 5:00 AM until 12:00 PM, cleaning up the Sears Department Store. Then, I would go home and sleep for a couple of hours.

After my rest, it would be time to head to my evening job at the United Parcel Service (UPS). I worked at UPS from 3:00 PM until 9:00 PM. My income, along with Denise's job at the phone company helped us pay the bills and continue to get by. Yet we were still living from paycheck to paycheck.

Determined to provide for my family, I made the two part-time jobs work for about a year and a half. In 1980, I heard that Thomas Jakes's mother, Mrs. Odith Jakes, was working at a job placement service. She had gotten a reputation for helping people get jobs. She didn't just get people jobs; she got them good paying jobs. I knew she would remember me and I was convinced that she would be willing to help me out of my financial predicament.

The day I went to see Mrs. Jakes I was a little nervous. I knew she was the perfect person to help steer me in the right direction. Therefore, I was very serious about my meeting with her. I prepared to see her just like I would have prepared for a job interview.

I had on some nice slacks and a dress shirt; I made sure that I looked my best. The minute she laid eyes on me, she flashed a big grin my way. *"Hello, Holloway,"* she said as I pulled up a chair to her desk. *"Hello, Mrs. Jakes,"* I responded as I leaned across the desk to greet her with a handshake. We exchanged pleasantries. Then I explained to her my search for full-time employment.

Looking over a sheet of paper on her desk, she began to talk to me about possible employment opportunities. All of a sudden, she came across one job that seemed to bring a twinkle to her eyes. Peering over the top of her glasses she said, *"There is a natural gas company that is hiring, but it is manual labor. You have to lay gas pipelines, work on streets, and bust concrete."*

She paused and added, *"but it pays well and the benefits are good too."*

Once she said, *"good pay and benefits"* in the same sentence, she had my undivided attention. *"What do I have to do,"* I asked. I knew a job like this might require experience I didn't have.

Mrs. Jakes pushed her chair back from her desk and looked me straight in the eyes and said, *"Holloway, all you have to do is sell yourself. If the man asks you what you are capable of, share with him what you can do. No matter what, you have to show that you are confident and you can do the job."*

As she handed me the referral, she said, *"I know you can do it. You just have to make sure that they know you can do it."* Taking the paper in my hand, I responded, *"Yes, ma'am."* Mrs. Jakes was a natural-born encourager. When I left her office, I was flying on cloud nine. I felt like the job was mine, all I needed to do was go for the interview.

Two days later I went for the job interview. In the back of my mind, I kept hearing Mrs. Jakes voice saying, *"sell yourself."* I knew this was what I was going to have to do. I put on my best clothes and I tried to look like somebody they would want working for their company. The gentleman who interviewed me began to fire questions at me, like a pitcher throwing balls in the World Series. I was ready for him. As soon as he would ask something, I would fire back a response.

To my surprise, they didn't ask me to return for a second interview. Instead, they hired me right on the spot.
A few days later, I stopped by the office to let Mrs. Jakes know her words of wisdom had gone a long way and I landed the job. When I told her the news, she just smiled at me and said, *"I knew that you could do it."*

* Uncovering The Past *

I sighed with relief once I landed the job with Mountaineer Gas Company. However, just as one aspect of my life was settling, another part of my life was falling apart. Even though Denise and I lived together before, she did not know how bad my drug addiction was until after we were married. She knew I had smoked pot and popped pills, but she had no idea I was shooting dope every chance I could get. I'm sure she knew something was wrong, but she couldn't quite put her finger on it.

When we were living together, I managed to keep the severity of my addiction from her. I think if she had known how strung-out I was early on, she might have reconsidered getting married. Once she found out what was really going on, she let me know she didn't want any part of it. With that being said, I tried to keep the hard stuff out of her sight, but after a while I just couldn't keep it from her any longer. My addiction had begun to take over my life.

H.G.

I have to admit in the beginning things were nice, but as my addiction got worse, our problems got worse.

Denise and I began to get into fights and arguments over little things, and then they would just escalate. It all boiled down to one thing: I was not standing up to my responsibilities. Even though I was married, there was a part of me that still wanted to be single. I wanted to hang out and kick it with the guys. At the time, I knew what I was doing was wrong, but I just didn't care to change.

Yet, there were times that my conscience began to bother me. For a while, I would straighten up and act right and when I was on point, the house was peaceful. Once I stepped out of place, everything around me fell apart. I would go on binges for weeks. If I was on a binge, the entire house was a chaotic mess.

* <u>Living</u> <u>As An</u> <u>Addict</u> *

After a while, I had to admit this wasn't just a kid phase that I was going through. I had a serious problem. I used both heroin and cocaine. The combination of the two was called "speed balling." I remember almost overdosing while shooting up once, but a buddy of mine brought me back. I was living my life so close to the edge that at any given moment I could have easily fallen off. This is how it is when you live that lifestyle; it is the only way that you know.

I learned to adapt my drug addiction to my life. I had heard stories about people who have been strung out on drugs, and they didn't work. The funny thing about it was, I was a working addict.

When I got the job at the gas company, I knew it was a good job and I wasn't about to mess it up for anything. We had our second child by this time; we named her Dana S. Gray. I went to work and I made provisions for my family. I faithfully continued to pay the bills, but at the same time I still had a very serious problem.

I remember on several occasions, I would give Denise half of my paycheck on Friday evening after I got off work. Then early Saturday morning around 3:00 AM, I would slip in her purse and steal back half the money I had just given her a few hours earlier. It's almost embarrassing to say that now, but that is the truth.

The next day when she got up, she would ask me if I knew what happened to the money I had given her. I would act like I didn't have a clue what she was talking about. I would just remind her that I wasn't at home when the money came up missing.

Denise is a smart woman; I think in the back of her head, she had to have known that it was me. Finally, it got so bad that she started hiding the money from me. One night, I went looking for the money I had given her earlier that day. I checked in the side pocket of her purse where she always put it, but it wasn't there. I knew then that Denise had gotten wise to my games.

Yet, that didn't stop me from doing my dirt. It didn't even slow me down. I just knew that source had dried up. I was going to get high and I didn't care how I got the money. While I continued to do drugs, I went through some hard and challenging times. My addiction made me steal from people that I knew, and lie to people that I loved.

In my heart, I wanted to do the right thing, but I just couldn't. I was like a puppet on a string. I would go anywhere that cocaine and heroin could pull me. I would chase anything I thought could lead me to my next high. Even though there wasn't an end in sight, there was something deep in my soul that still wanted to do right.

A typical day for me would begin by getting up and taking a shower, but because I was down from the night before, I would also take something to bring me up. Before even sitting down at the table for breakfast, I would have already popped an upper or two. Then, I would eat some breakfast and go to work. We worked as a chain gang, of sorts, as we would fix pipelines as a group. Our work could go from fixing a two to three-inch pipe to installing a twenty-inch pipeline.

When I got to work, things were free-flowing. I would get with a couple of guys on the job and the next thing I knew someone would pull out a joint. Most times we would go smoke it before we even started work. Being high didn't make a difference. We still got the work done.

Of course, my co-workers knew I was getting high. What they didn't know was that on any given day I might also have a syringe stashed away in my socks.

By mid-day, my high would have worn off. I would separate myself from the group so I could go to the restroom and take care of my business. Once I got in the restroom, I would remove the syringe from my sock and give myself a shot in the arm. Moments later, I would head back to work.

If the workload was heavy, we could work another twelve hours that day. I would actually keep something with me all day to keep me going. I was a functioning addict, but an addict nonetheless.

When I started to look at the results of some of my actions, it bothered me. I couldn't believe I allowed myself to stoop that low. I was letting down the people I loved the most. I was stealing from those who were the closest to me, and causing pain to my family.

My lifestyle made me lie, manipulate, steal and cheat. I was hurting myself and I was hurting those around me. The pain was multi-faceted. After a while, my actions began to take a toll on me. For some people it might have been nothing, but for me the way I treated those I loved was everything. Even though my drug use was out of control, my actions made me consider what my addiction was doing to me. I thought it was pretty brutal for me to stoop that low.

After doing this for several years, I was convinced my company was going to find out about my addiction. I couldn't keep it from my family; and it was a matter of time before my job would know as well. I didn't know if they would find out, I may have just been paranoid. So I figured, the best thing for me to do was let them know I had a problem before they came to me about it. Since there were a few of us that were known to use drugs, it seemed like it would only be a matter of time before someone found out.

I thought coming forward would be the best way for me to save my job and save my family. I didn't want to be looked at as one that wasn't making provisions for his family. After a while, I began to feel like the handwriting was on the wall. If I kept doing drugs, I was going to be unemployed.

When I admitted to the company I had a problem, the company put me in a treatment center for about a month. My thirty-day stay cost them around thirty thousand dollars. It was expensive to be an addict, and even more costly to kick the habit. However, I knew I needed to do something. I couldn't keep on the way I was going.

I stayed clean for about six months. One of my biggest problems was simple; I couldn't separate myself from my friends. I still had to kick it with the fellas. I thought I was fine. I didn't think there was any harm just going out with them like we had always done. After all, I was clean now. We all went to the bars, but I only drank coke. I was able to do that for a while.

Eventually I would come across days that seemed to be a little tough to get through, but there was one day that was particularly bad. I ended up going to the bar with the guys as usual. This time, instead of having a coke I had a drink. A drink went to taking a pill. The pill led to taking a shot. The shot led to me getting back on the roller coaster ride that my company had spent thirty thousand dollars to get me off of. In no time at all, I was in the same boat I had been in for years. It was almost as if I had never stopped.

I have heard people say that once you've done drugs, if you go back to it at a later time, it is almost like you've never missed a beat. That was so true. After experiencing the relapse, I was back in the same situation and playing the same old games for another couple of years. I knew the next time it would take more than money to get me back on track.

* Scripture Reference

"Two are better than one, because they have a good reward for their labor. For if they fall, one will lift up his companion. But woe to him who is alone when he falls, for he has no one to help him up. Again, if two lie down together, they will keep warm; but how can one be warm alone?"

Ecclesiastes 4:9-11 (KJV)

* Prayer

Lord, I know that You have a divine connection for me. Please allow me to realize the person You would have me be in partnership with. Reveal my destiny relation, so I do not continue to stumble alone in the darkness of life.

CHAPTER SEVEN

A Change of Direction: God Heals My Addiction

"Every problem is an opportunity to know God better, and our primary battle is to know God well."

~Dr. Robert Kellemen

When I really began to hit rock bottom, Denise and I were both young. We were in our late-twenties and we had taken a taste of the good life. We were both driving nice cars; we had good jobs and we were living large. I was also doing a few things on the side to make a little extra money.

We both liked the nightlife, and we would party hard on the weekends. I had my own little hustle going on the side to keep cash flowing. I kept money in my pocket and cocaine in my nose.

Living that type of lifestyle made me feel like I was invincible sometimes; other times I felt like I was out of control. There was no doubt that drugs distorted my reality.

I distinctly remember one night that Denise and I went out to this hot nightspot. I had been shooting and snorting cocaine earlier that evening. I was flying high when we walked in the club, and the lights were laying low. Once I got in the club, something happened. Even though I had been wanting to party, I started feeling weird. The music was loud and people were getting their groove on, but something just didn't feel right for me. I wasn't sure if it was just the paranoia from the drugs or what. All of sudden, I started to have an anxiety attack. I just did not want to be there.

Denise could tell by looking at my face that something was wrong with me. She patted me on the arm and said, "*Baby, wait right here. I am going to get the car,*" but when she left me, the cocaine hit me like a brick wall. I started to lose it. Even though she told me she was going to get the car, I didn't have a clue where she was. I completely lost my composure. I started to freak out.

It just so happened that some of our friends were there as well. One of them grabbed me by the arm and said, *"Denise is gone man, but she is going to be right back."* He was trying to assure me that everything was going to be okay, but his assurance wasn't working. The cocaine was stronger than his rationale.

I was so stressed out that I broke out in a cold sweat. As beads of water the size of gumballs were running off of my head, it was obvious to my friend that his words were not calming me. Finally, someone tapped me on the shoulder and said, *"We got you, Holloway."* To this day, I don't know how I got out of the club that night. I realize that Denise must have returned, but the rest of the night was a complete blur for me.

I know now that when you have a night like that, it is a sign that something is really wrong in your life. I had plenty of money, a lot of drugs, and I was having a good time, but I still had bad experiences.

As I searched for clues on how I got in the predicament I was in, I realized that something changed. This all started out as fun: the lifestyle, the flowing cash and living large. It was all fun at first, but at some point during my journey, the fun left. I can't tell you when it left, but I can tell you that it did. When all the fun was gone, it was replaced with pain and agony. It didn't happen overnight, but over time, the rules of the game changed. I was no longer a major player, but a pawn on a chessboard being moved from place to place.

After a while, it seemed I had been moved so far out of place that I might never get back in position. By the time I felt I had reached a place of no return, Denise and I were staying in a complex called the Roxalana Hills Apartments. I came home late one night and I had been drinking. I was at the bottom of a hill and I had no idea where I was going or what I was doing. Needless to say, this was not the time to be behind the wheel of car, but I was.

My vision was impaired, and all I could see was one car coming up the road and another one going down the road. I must have turned too quick to avoid the car coming toward me. Before I knew it, my car lunged forward. I drove into the median, which separated the two lanes of the road.

Instead of colliding with a pole or another car, my car was perfectly placed in the cement island between the two roads. All night I remained there on the thin strip of cement that divided the two lanes of traffic. This scenario was almost indicative of my life. I was stuck in the middle with no viable way out.

I don't know what happened from that point on. I just passed out. The next thing I knew, I woke up with my head resting on the steering wheel. I glanced around, and it was daylight. There was not any broken glass, no sirens or emergency vehicles. To my amazement, it was just me.

I had no clue on how I got there, but it looked like someone had placed me there for my own protection. As I evaluated the situation, I knew this was a miracle, that I had not killed anyone else or been killed.

Even though I was not shooting dope that night, the simple fact that I was drunk was enough to have caused some major damage. It was almost incomprehensible that I had made it only a few blocks from home before this incident had occurred.

I had no idea how long I had been there. I couldn't believe someone had not called the police. I knew I could have easily been arrested, but being arrested was the least of my problems. It was evident that this incident could have been fatal.

This was a life changing moment for me. I knew that something had to give. Something had to change. I had been dancing with darkness long enough. There was no doubt in my mind I needed deliverance. Old habits do die hard, but at some point everything must die.

I knew I had to get back to God; I no longer had an option. The Spirit of God had been speaking to me in a small voice all my life. All I could hope for was the whispers in my spirit to be stronger than the ghosts in my past.

I knew I had been raised in the church and this was my redeeming factor. I still had something to fall back on when everything around me was falling apart. I know so many people who did not have anything to fall back on, and they never made it out of their addiction. Many of them are not here today, but I thank God this is not my testimony.

No matter how hard I tried to hide from it, my addiction had begun to hang around my neck like a noose. The more I got into it, the tighter the rope got. Many times I found myself gasping for air. It felt like I was chasing something every day and I couldn't seem to catch it, but every day I was still chasing it. By the end of the day, I would get my high and then I would get my fix. Each day I woke up, the cycle started all over again, and the chase was on. It was almost like a never-ending cycle. I realized how this thing worked and knew that the race was fixed; there was no way that I could win.

In the midst of being strung out, I began to ask God, *"when?"* I knew that I couldn't continue like this anymore. I knew it had to come to an end someday; I just wanted to know – when? In my soul, I began to cry out, *"When, Lord, when?"* I never felt like I got an answer. There was just this undeniable silence. Yet, I did not stop asking the question.

Although I was still doing my dirt, I would find a way to go to church. I wouldn't go every Sunday; I would go to church every now and then. I attended a Baptist church that our family had always gone to when I was growing up.

Some of my friends used to call me "Way" as a short for Holloway. One of my old buddies teased me, he said, " *Way, the funny thing about when we were growing up was with all the trouble we got into, you always found your way back to church for some reason or another."* He was right. This time I wasn't strong enough to get to the church. I needed the church to come to me.

One evening when we were still living in the Roxalana Hills Apartments, Denise was getting ready to go out for a night on the town with her girlfriends. I didn't mind; I just wanted a little peace and quiet while the kids stayed with my sister.

Once Denise left, there was a heaviness that came over me. It was almost like a deep depression. I just felt this internal exhaustion. I tried to watch television, but I just couldn't shake it. I didn't feel suicidal or anything, but something inside kept saying this has to come to an end.

I couldn't think of anything else to do that would bring me peace, so I decided to take a bath. I ran the water until it got as hot as I could stand it. I submerged my body in the hot water, and rested my head on the back of the tub. As I sunk down under the water, I became overwhelmed with emotions. As I laid there, my entire body began to throb. I began to feel pain from the top of my head to the tip of my baby toe. My entire body ached. I had never experienced pain like this in my life. I needed some relief and I didn't know what to do. Then I realized that Denise wasn't home. Who in the world was going to help me get out this pain?

At that point, I remembered back to the little boy sitting on the back of the church pew. There was nobody there physically to help me. I needed Jesus! As I began to beg for relief from the Lord, tears started to roll down my checks. I cried out to the Lord in agony, *"When, when, when Lord, when?"* When would I stop this viscous cycle? When would I get off this roller coaster ride that I had been on for over a decade and a half? When would I become the man that God created me to be?

My body was so overcome with pain that everything in me started to shut down. The only thing working was my mind. I began to have a very vivid picture of my life. I saw the young boy taking his first drink. I saw the teenager sitting in the back of the classroom stoned out of his mind. I saw the man in the bathroom, sticking a needle in his arm. Then I saw the man passed out in the car, in the middle of the road.

Without a lot of fanfare and long drawn out words, in that moment I asked God to come back into my heart. I had finally come to the crossing point in the road. This time, I let out one last cry, *"When?"*

Finally, I got my answer. It was like something from a movie. I could literally feel the room spinning, although I wasn't drinking or using drugs. The roller coaster ride I had been on for over sixteen years of my life was about to come to a screeching halt. I gripped the side of the tub with my fingers; I had no idea what was going to happen next. I was having a come to Jesus meeting right in the privacy of my own bathroom. There was no preacher, no pastor, not even a psalmist. There was just one simple prayer, for God to change my life. He finally answered my question *"when"*, with the simple word: *"Now!"*

In minutes, God did what a trip to a rehabilitation center could not do. He began to clean me up, this time from the inside out. He began to wash away the sting of the streets, the lingering lies, and the mastered manipulation.

I knew then that God truly had heard me. I immediately felt a relief from my pain that night. I realized the pain that I had felt in my body was a symbol of the pain that was plaguing my soul. I had been caring the weight of the world on my shoulders, and it was just too much for me to bear. Jesus said, *"My yoke is easy and my burdens are light."*

When I let the water out of the bathtub, every pore of my body was tingling with relief. As the water drained, I couldn't help imagining that it was taking with it some of the dirt I had been trying to get rid of for sixteen years. On that particular night, God gave me a peace that would be with me for the rest of my life. As I dried myself off and prepared for bed, I tried to comprehend what just happened to me, but there were no words to describe it.

A few hours later, Denise came home. She definitely had a good time with her friends because she was a little tipsy. I wanted to say something to her, but the Holy Spirit said, *"Don't say a thing."* I just helped her get her things off and put her to bed. I kissed her on the forehead as she slipped under the covers. I knew that our lives were about to change.

That Sunday I could not wait to go to church. I needed to seal the deal with God. He had started a work with me and I wanted to finish it. At the end of the service, I went up to the front of the church to rededicate my life to the Lord. This time it was not just out of tradition; it was a soul commitment.

From that point on, God let me know I needed to be an example for my household. So, I became an example for my wife and my children. Once God did a work in me, He began to do a work in everyone around me. It didn't just include Denise, but my sisters and my brother as well. He delivered me, and then He began to deal with everyone connected to me.

I have to admit, that night in the bathroom I got sick and tired of being sick and tired. I knew I could not continue to chase something I could not catch. The mood swings, the dysfunction, and the self-destruction; it all had to die so that I might live. My condition had affected everyone I came in contact with, and hurt everyone that was close to me.
To this day, I thank God for reconciliation, forgiveness and compassion. He saved me, and then He restored me.

When I asked God to come back in my heart, there weren't any great words that I said; it was just the Spirit of God that I felt in my heart. Once I felt His presence, I knew that the shackles had fallen off. Over the years, I knew there was a lot of weight on me. For most of my life, I tried to live up to a lifestyle that wasn't really made for me. It was a lifestyle that I tried to put before my friends and family. I thought it was great and glamorous but it really wasn't.

For the first six years of our marriage, the time had gone by so slow. There were weeks and months I didn't even remember, but to this day, I wouldn't change anything. Those trials and tribulations helped to make us who we are today.

My love for Denise has totally intensified because I knew there were so many times she could have left, but she chose to stay. She made a commitment not only to me but also to the marriage. For me, her dedication spoke volumes to our relationship. She wanted to make it work and that made me want to make it work even more.

Denise saw something in me no one else did. Her love made me want to step up to the plate and be a different man. God's love for me made me want to step up to the plate and be a better person.

Now, I had reached a turning point in my life. I knew many of my friends did not have the same Christian background I grew up with. Therefore, they didn't have anything to fall back on. It became my obligation to share and show them the way. This is reflected by my life and the lifestyle I live now. My hope and prayer is they see something so appealing in me; it will cause them to want to change. I want them to experience Jesus Christ in me, by my every day walk with Him. When I stopped running toward what I couldn't catch, God caught me. Then He changed me.

* Scripture Reference

"And one shall say, Heap it up! Heap it up! Prepare the way,
Take the stumbling block out of the way of My people."

Isaiah 57:14 (KJV)

* Prayer

Lord, I have hit rock bottom in my life. I know no one can reach me where You can reach me. I don't need a physical healing; I need a soul connection. I need You to touch my soul and heal my inner being. I want to be the person You have called me to be.

CHAPTER EIGHT

Ordered Footsteps:
A New Church Home

"God moves in mysterious ways. His wonders to perform; He plants his footsteps in the sea and rides upon the storm."
~William Cowper

The night in the tub was a life-changing event for me. After that night, I allowed God to come back into my life. I will never forget it; it was on a Friday evening. Two days later, I was in church. My heart had been hurting for so long, the pain began to feel normal to me. I was exhausted from running after something that was out of my reach. I was constantly trying to recapture that first high, but I was never going to get it. In the process, I was ruining my life and destroying everything around me.

There was no doubt I was in a losing battle. It was like being in a boxing ring with an invisible contender; with no way to win. Life was giving me an upper cut to the left and a jab to the right. As soon as I bounced back, there was another sharp jab to the left. I knew in the back of my mind that this vicious cycle was going to have to come to an end. I no longer wanted to play games with God, because my arms were too short to box with Him.

This time, I had to be strong enough to get out of the ring and step into the real world. Deep in my heart I knew God was calling me to a deeper place. I wanted to serve Him the right way. I was no longer content with giving Him what was left; I needed to give Him my best. I wanted the Lord to have the main course. I wanted to serve Him to the best of my abilities for the rest of my life.

The more I thought about it, the more I realized that all my life I had been trying to live up to a standard I could not achieve. As a child when I was in the church, it seemed challenging to walk with Christ. The harder I tried, the more I seemed to fall by the wayside. For me, serving God was like trying to walk on a tight rope. No matter how hard I tried, I just couldn't do it. There was something inside of me that wanted to do right. I really wanted to be right in the sight of God. I just couldn't accomplish it the way the church was telling me I needed to do it.

This time when I returned to the church, I felt as if God was giving me a new lease on life. I still remember standing in front of the church after I rededicated my life back to God. I had tears running down my face, and my heart was wide open. I didn't want to do this my way; I wanted to do it God's way.

After I joined the Church, Denise followed in my footsteps. We both got involved right away. Denise sang in the choir, and I worked on the usher board. Somehow in serving God, I began to surrender. As I continued to volunteer, God began to do a new work in my life. I no longer had to try to keep myself because God began to keep me.

Nearly four years had passed by when something started to change in me. I am not sure what happened, but God began to drop in my spirit the words, *"Temple of Faith."* It was so strong when I first heard it; I jumped up and turned around. I knew someone had to be speaking to me. I could hear it as clear as day. Then, I heard the words: *"Temple of Faith, T. D. Jakes."*

For the life of me, I couldn't figure it out. At first I thought this was just my flesh speaking to me. My childhood friend, Thomas was preaching at Temple of Faith. Maybe something inside me just wanted to attend his church.

After a while I couldn't shake it, I began to question God. What was He trying to say to me? What did this mean? Why was He dropping Temple of Faith in my spirit with such intensity? I didn't have answers to all my questions, but I have learned over the years God always has a plan.
He began to give me a greater desire to want more of Him. I was just not content with going to church anymore; I wanted all that God had to offer me.

The more I thirsted after God; the more I paid attention to my surroundings. I started paying attention to people I knew who were supposed to be Christians. There was this guy I worked with at the gas company. His name was Jim. He was a real good friend of mine. I knew there was something different about Jim. His walk with God was different than my walk.

Overall, I had a genuine respect for him. Some guys I worked with would call themselves Christians, but they would curse you out in a minute. Some of them would also keep pornography in their trucks, but Jim wasn't that kind of guy. There was no doubt in my mind that Jim was a godly man who was filled with the Holy Ghost.

I began to seek God on what made us so different. We were both Christians, and we were both men. I couldn't quite put my finger on it. I just knew there was an undeniable difference between us. Then one day, Jim invited me to a prayer breakfast. It was the Full Gospel Businessmen's Prayer Breakfast. There were a lot of Caucasian men there, but not too many African American men.

During the breakfast, they began to talk about being filled with the Holy Ghost and I became curious. One of the guys stood up and asked, *"Does anyone want to be filled with the Holy Spirit?"* He then explained, *"If you just come up, we are going to touch and agree with you. We'll believe God, and watch Him work."*

Determined to get all that God had for me, I went up to the front with a few other guys. The gentleman who was speaking began to go in depth about speaking in tongues, he said, *"You may not speak in tongues the first time. We really don't know when you will speak in tongues, but we do know that God will fill you if you ask Him."*

His words seemed plain and simple. All I could hear him saying was, *"He will fill you, if you ask Him."* This was enough for me. I threw my hands up in the air and asked God to fill me with the Holy Ghost, but nothing happened.

A couple of weeks later Jim and I were working on the same truck together. It just happened to be National Prayer Day. It was early in the morning. We were in this big, old gas truck going on a drill, and Jim looked at me and said, *"Let's start the day off right. Why don't we have a morning prayer as we are going down the road?"*

I had never done this before, but I was open to anything that seemed like God. I just said, *"Sounds good to me, doc."* As we drove down the road, Jim started praying. While he was praying, I began to agree with him in the spirit. Jim was really going in. He said, *"Heavenly father, we ask You to just let Your blessing rain down upon us on this day."*

I think before he even got the word "blessing" out of his mouth, something happened. It was as if the heavens opened up and welcomed Jim's words. I knew the road was bumpy, but the truck began to rock. It almost felt as if a lightning bolt hit the side of the truck, Bam! The Holy Spirit came in the truck and filled me instantly. Right then and there I began to speak in tongues.

It wasn't a fancy church service or a great gathering of people. It was just Jim and I. God showed up, and He showed out. I began to wave my hands in the air. I was so excited. Once I was able to speak in English again, *"Oh my God,"* was all I could say. I had never experienced anything like that before in my life. It was a new high, but this time it was real. I didn't have to take anything to make it happen, God facilitated all of it.

Jim pulled the truck over to the side of the road. It was like an old fashion hoedown. We both jumped out of the truck and started dancing and rejoicing. Out in the middle of the field among the trees and all of God's nature, we were praising the Lord with all our hearts. God had revealed Himself to me in a new way, and it made all the difference in world.

I was so excited about this experience that I could not wait to tell my pastor about it. To my surprise, it didn't seem like a big deal to him. In fact, he was somewhat nonchalant about it. I'd just had an experience of a lifetime and for him it was just mediocre.

At first, I couldn't understand it. Then I realized what I had experienced was different. Our church was still hung up on tradition. When I realized my pastor's response was based on tradition, I had my answer on what to do next. I knew why God had been putting Temple of Faith in my spirit. It was time for me to step out of my comfort zone and into a God zone. If I was going to reach the next level, I had to experience something new.

* Scripture Reference

"Jesus answered and said unto her, 'Whosoever drinketh of this water shall thirst again: But whosoever drinketh of the water that I shall give him shall never thirst; but the water that I shall give him shall be in him a well of water springing up into everlasting life.'"

John 4: 13-14 (KJV)

* Prayer

Lord, my soul is thirsty. I ask that You fill me from your everlasting fountain. Plant me in a place that will saturate my soul and I may flow with the Holy Spirit. Immerse my spiritual roots in a soil that will enrich me from the inside out. Let me find a church home that will allow me to drink from Your cup, so I will never run dry.

CHAPTER NINE

Destiny Steps

When God is calling you to a path toward greatness, it doesn't mean that the course is cleared of obstacles. In fact, the greater your calling -- the greater the struggle.

~Joel Osteen

I heard Thomas Jakes was going to be preaching at a local church near our community. This news excited me. Although it had been nearly twenty years since I'd seen him, he was always a friend in my heart. How could I forget him, it was Mrs. Jakes who helped me get the job with Mountaineer Gas. I was just talking to my wife, Denise about him. I was telling her that he was my best friend when I was a kid. It was hard to believe this little boy who'd befriended me was now a minister. I always knew there was something different about him. Now, I just had to see him again.

It seemed like the week flew by as Denise and I made plans to hear Thomas preach. When I thought about seeing him again, my mind began to race with questions. What had he been doing? What made him decide to become a preacher? Would he even remember me?

Finally, the night had come and we were on our way to see my old friend. To our disbelief, Denise and I realized we had the times mixed up. By the time we arrived at the church, the service was over and Thomas was greeting the people in the audience. There was no missing him. At 6"3, he towered over people. It was amazing to see how he graciously moved through the crowd as they anxiously gathered around him. As I looked around the room it was obvious that his sermon was well received. Many people even waited after service just to shake his hand.

As a long line formed to greet the man of God, Denise and I positioned ourselves at the end of the line. We wanted to make sure we had an opportunity to extend our well wishes to him. The closer we moved up in the line, the more I realized that time had matured Thomas. Even so, I could still see that little boy with those all-knowing eyes.

Finally the line dwindled down to just us, and after almost two decades apart, there we were, standing face to face. I extended my hand toward his and he grabbed it with a firm grip. I looked straight into his eyes and said, *"Thomas Jakes"*. I didn't attach elder or any other title to my friend who had turned preacher.

He responded, *"Holloway Gray"*. The twenty years of separation quickly vanished and I was back with my childhood friend. As soon as I shook his hand, it immediately took me back to old times. From that point on, formalities went out of the window.

We embraced each other. We hugged. We laughed. All the questions that had been pinned up inside of me began to flow. It was almost like a David and Jonathan experience. We were kindred brothers reconnected by the Spirit. Although we were apart for a long time, there was something that was drawing us back together again and that something was bigger than the both of us.

It didn't take me long to realize that he was no longer just my playground friend. He had changed quite a bit, but there were still some things about him that had not changed at all. He was still so friendly. He wasn't at all condemning or judgmental either. He had a certain disposition about him that was unlike anyone else I knew. As soon as I looked into his eyes, God began to show me and reveal to me things that He would begin to do. There are no words to describe it but something in me was rekindled. Even though I couldn't verbalize it, there was something in me that felt there would be more to come. Finally, I introduced him to Denise. We discussed church a little and told him where we attended. He invited us to worship with him sometime if possible, and I assured him we would. Then we parted ways once again.

I didn't know when I would see Thomas again, but I knew our next meeting would be inevitable. Denise and I laughed all the way home as we reflected on me being reunited with my childhood friend. However, I knew deep down inside that this was not an ordinary meeting, but would be the beginning of destiny and fate lining up in my life. The little boy that used to have dreams and aspirations was now reborn.

* Scripture Reference

"And it came to pass, when he had made an end of speaking unto Saul, that the soul of Jonathan was knit with the soul of David, and Jonathan loved him as his own soul."

1 Samuel 18:1 KJV

God has a divine plan for your life. No matter what you have been through or what you are going through, He is orchestrating your journey. Soon, your past and your present will intersect on the line of destination.

* Prayer

Lord, give me a revelation of how You have strategically orchestrated the steps of my journey. Please remove any blinders that have hindered me from seeing Your ultimate guidance in my life.

I thank You for those You have positioned in my pathway to push me into my destiny. Let my next step be my greatest, because I am relinquishing me and relying on You.

CHAPTER TEN

A Breath Of
Fresh Air

"Efforts and courage are not enough without

purpose and direction."

~John F. Kennedy

A few years had gone by and I was in a new place with God. My walk was getting stronger by the day. Denise and I were faithfully serving in our church and I knew a change was about to come. Gwen, a friend of Denise and I, invited us to attend a service at Temple of Faith. Of course, I jumped at the opportunity. This was where my friend, Thomas Jakes, pastored.

Temple of Faith was in Montgomery, West Virginia, which is a little bit north of Charleston. It was about a forty-five minute drive for us. I was looking forward to going. I was so hungry for Christ; I wanted more of Him and I had heard all the wonderful things God was doing at this church.

The service at Temple of Faith was on a spiritual high. It was nothing like I was accustomed to on a Sunday morning at my church. It was different, but it was refreshing. Nothing about it was traditional. The Holy Spirit seemed to have free reign there. Even though the service had order, you could sense in the air that God was the most important thing on the agenda.

After service, I had to catch my breath. I couldn't believe that God had moved so freely throughout the entire service. I was baffled by the experience. I asked, Gwen, *"Does this happen every Sunday?"*

By the look on her face, I could tell she was just waiting for me to ask that question. Without a doubt, she said, *"Yes, child."* Then she continued to brag about the type of worship experience they had at Temple of Faith on a regular basis. I just looked at Gwen in complete dismay. I thought for sure she was lying.

I knew what I had experienced was real. I could not believe they had that kind of service every single Sunday. There was just no way. It was impossible. The church we attended was a Baptist church, and we didn't have service like that every Sunday.

I was sure Gwen was just bragging. I looked her straight in the eyes, and said, *"You mean the Spirit moves in your church like this every Sunday?"* Without blinking her eyes, Gwen responded, *"Every Sunday."*

Denise and I cordially said our good-byes to Gwen and her husband, West. Then we got in the car. I couldn't wait until the door closed. I said, *"Denise, you know, I just don't believe Gwen. I think she is lying,"* trying to get a grasp on what we had just encountered.

Little did I realize, Gwen was telling the truth. We returned to Temple of Faith a few Sundays later. The same thing happened. The service was still very high, and God was moving in a mighty way.

By this time, I could not get Temple of Faith out of my head and I didn't know what to do. I started to argue with God because I had no idea how I would ever convince Denise to make a move like this. Then before I could even contemplate the question of how to tell Denise, God said, *"I got this."* Once God spoke to me, I knew I had to move. I had to trust He was going to orchestrate everything else.

One day, I decided to confront Denise with the issue. I said, *"Honey, you know what? Something has been on my heart for a while. God dropped in my spirit, Temple of Faith – T.D Jakes."* With a twinkle in her eyes, she responded, *"Really?"*

She knew Bishop was a childhood friend of mine, and she'd met him personally a few years prior. However, Denise is not a woman who is easily persuaded, so I began to prepare my next plan of action in case she shut it down.

I thought for sure, she would have asked an array of questions like...what, when and how? Surprisingly, she didn't say any of that. In fact, she was so open and submitted. Her response was very simple, *"Tell me when."* She then added, *"I am with you, Holloway."*

I was so flabbergasted to see how God had worked it out, without any help from me. I just couldn't believe it. We were both on one accord about the move. We came up with a plan to go to our pastor and tell him we were getting ready to make a change. In the meantime, we went back to visit Temple of Faith one more time.

We got the letter of resignation together to give to our pastor. Then, we went to meet with Bishop and Mrs. Jakes to inform them we were coming to their church. We didn't just want to come in without everyone being aware of our intent.

Even though I was raised in a very traditional Baptist Church, there was still something righteous about it. Therefore, I felt compelled to do things decently and in order.

The Sunday we left our old church, there wasn't a dry eye in the house. I had grown up in this church. Denise and I both were very active there. Every one cried so much we thought they would have to build an ark in the middle of the sanctuary. We loved the people, and they loved us. It was the only church we really knew.

Change is not always easy, especially when you're not in control of it. Deep in my heart, I knew it was time for a change, but I had no idea what to expect next. Denise and I were stepping out of the familiar and into the unknown. We were both about to embark on one of the greatest challenges of our lives, as God was pushing me into my destiny.

* Scripture Reference

"By faith Abraham, when he was called to go out into a place which he should after receive for an inheritance, obeyed; and he went out, not knowing whither he went."

Hebrews 11:8 (KJV)

Many times, change comes in our life like a strong wind. It is not what we want, but it is what we need.

* Prayer

Lord, please allow me to be open to the changes that You have ordained for my life. Don't allow me to become stagnant in the status quo and settle for less than what You have for me. Let me delight myself in You, as I embrace Your direction for my life. I realize that with You as my guide, the best is yet to come.

CHAPTER ELEVEN

A Path For Success: Working At Temple of Faith

"Now the only way you can serve God on earth

is by serving others."

~Rick Warren

When you put a plant in the right soil, it flourishes. Once Denise and I got to Temple of Faith, we did just that. Our roots were immersed deep in the foundation of the church; the word that went forth was like water to our souls. Worshiping in that environment was so refreshing and rejuvenating. There is no other way to put it; the church was just exciting. The Holy Ghost filled the atmosphere to the point where it was simply electrifying. There was a certain level of expectancy that was always in the air.

I think one of the things that made the church unique was "truth." It was constantly going forth. It was as if the mailman was dropping off mail every week. There were no exceptions. Each Sunday you could expect to get a fresh word straight from heaven. What made the experience seem remarkable that the word always seemed custom designed just for you. No matter what you were going through or what you had gone through that week, the word fit your situation.

From the choir to the back of the church, there was a divine connection. Everything and everyone seemed to be joined together like a well-woven fabric. This was a totally new experience for Denise and I and we were definitely up for it. Even though our trip from home was a thirty-mile drive one way, it was nothing to us. The difference was worth the distance. There was one thing we both knew: the Holy Ghost was in charge at the Temple of Faith, and we wanted to be welcomed participants.

I loved the fact that there was always order at the church. Yet, God had free reign. It was evident that Elder Jakes had a keen awareness for the presence of God. He was very sensitive to the Spirit of the Lord showing up in the service. Knowing the Holy Ghost was going to be present in the service was such a big plus for us. Sometimes He would show up at the beginning of service, or right in the middle. Other times He may not show up until the end of the service. The one thing you could count on for sure was before church ended; the anointing of the Holy Spirit was going to fill the place.

I was so grateful Elder Jakes had an ear to hear the voice of the Lord. He openly took direction from Him on how the service should flow every week. Everyone was so friendly. From the time you walked thru the doors of the church, there was this warmth that reached out and greeted you. The church was smaller than Shiloh Baptist Church but the size didn't matter to me. I think it just added to the closeness we all felt. It was more like being a part of a big family rather than joining a church. The church was just a building, but what we had was a relationship.

Temple of Faith met in an old converted movie theatre. The majority of the church was on the main floor. There was a small balcony, and a few additional rooms and that was it. Denise and I quickly learned that size was not everything. I just knew being a part of this church was going to change our lives; I could feel it.

This place truly had a unique anointing on it. The singing was better, the praying was better, the preaching was better and there was no doubt the anointing at Temple of Faith made the difference. When God's anointing is present it makes everything better.

For the first two years, Denise and I kept a relatively low profile. We were in no way as busy as we had been at our previous church. We went from being in the choir, serving on the usher board and helping the youth to doing absolutely nothing. During this time frame we were like dry sponges absorbing the Word of God each and every chance we got: Sunday mornings, Sunday nights, Wednesday evenings and whenever else we could get it.

It was obvious to us the church was full of purpose. The church members worked together to accomplish one goal and one mission. Their main purpose was saving souls and giving people what they needed.

The entire experience was something new for me; little did I realize that God was getting ready to do a new thing in my life. I couldn't understand it at the time, but for some reason God had me in an observation mode. I would just sit there in the pew and watch Elder Jakes as he delivered the word. I began to pay close attention to the details of his delivery. I examined the Spirit that rested on him. This was no longer my childhood friend. He was now my shepherd, and I was a faithful member of his flock.

Even though I really didn't understand, I just took everything in. As I watched him, I began to understand his character, his disposition, his style, and the way he delivered a message. I got a glimpse of how he operated under the anointing. After a while, it was like I could almost anticipate his next move.

God was giving me an uncanny ability to flow with him. It was almost like an Elijah and Elisha encounter.

As Denise and I began to settle in, we both felt compelled to give back to the church because it had been such a blessing to us. Even though I was still working at Mountaineer Gas Company, I wanted to see if any additional help was needed around the church. Sometimes when I would get off work, I would drive by to check on things. I would take out the trash, restock the toilet paper in the bathrooms, and clean up the pastor's office. After doing those things, I would sweep and mop to make sure things were kept clean. This just seemed like my reasonable service. After all, we were being fed there on a regular basis.

*God Uses Ordinary People to do Extraordinary Things *

After just sitting for a couple of years, Elder Jakes came to me one Sunday after service. He was soaking wet. He had preached so hard that perspiration was running from the top of his head down to the sole of his socks. You could see sweat marks under the arms pits of his light blue suit. He was so wet, his shoes literally squeaked when he walked.

In desperation, he handed me his clothes and asked me to help him get ready for his next event. I almost froze at his request. I had cleaned his office but the idea of helping him seemed like a job that was much bigger than I could handle. I had never done anything like this before. I had spent the last decade and a half digging ditches and running pipelines. How do you go from manual labor to supporting the Pastor? It was only by the grace of God.

Questions began to dodge around my mind, like ping -pong balls. What did he need? What to expect? I had no idea what to do. Was I nervous? Yeah, I was nervous. This was Elder Jakes. I wanted to make sure I did the right thing.

He made it all seem much easier, as he yelled out to me, "Grab my stuff." Then he instructed me where to lay his wet things. Before I knew it, I had developed a system to help him change and get ready for his next assignment. I was meticulous in the way I did things. I had spent time picking up on his mannerisms because I wanted to do things right. This was just the beginning of God preparing me to facilitate the needs of the ministry by serving the leader of the house. It was just a small assignment like this, which gave me basic preparation for what it would take to be an armor bearer and assist a great Man of God.

After I successfully completed the task, Elder Jakes asked me if I could help him on Sundays before and after service. He let me know it would be a tremendous help to him to have my assistance. In an instant, I went from taking out the trash to helping him stay on track as he ministered.

My assignment didn't just stop there, it was evident God saved me to serve. I became involved in every part of the ministry. I even began to help West duplicate the tapes in the audio room.

During this time, the Lord blessed Elder Jakes and he became ordained as a Bishop. As the ministry grew, he began to travel more. He would leave town on Tuesday and preach in cities across the country. Sometimes he would take stacks of fifty to one hundred tapes with him. He often spent a lot of time in neighboring cities that were close by like Toledo, Columbus and Dayton.

One Wednesday night, he called West about midnight. Bishop had just left to go out of town the night before and he was already out of tapes. When West got the news he called me and said, *"Hey Holloway, can you meet me at the church in a half an hour?"* Then he called Pam, and she also helped us. I was half asleep, but before I knew it I said, *"Yes."* Then I threw some clothes on and headed up to the church.

It was almost 12:45 AM by the time I got there, but I wasn't even tired. I knew we had a job to do. Pam arrived about fifteen minutes before I got there. That night we duplicated about three hundred tapes. We packaged them, put them in a box and headed to the airport. By the time we finished, it was about 4:00 AM. All of us had jobs to go to. We went home and got a little sleep. Before I knew it, it was time to get up for work. I jumped in the shower and got ready to start my day.

I stayed up all night when I was in the world, and I would be exhausted the next day. This time, I was full of energy because I was fulfilling a mission. I felt like I was helping move the purpose of the ministry forward. This was now bigger than me; it was actually a calling on my life.

West, Pam and I did this for years. The cities were different, the amount of tapes changed, but the mission was the same. We did what was needed and what was required. We didn't grumble and we didn't complain. We just did it. In fact, we felt privileged to do it. Was it hard? Yes, it was hard. Was it worth it? Yes, it was worth it. Helping the ministry grow was one of the most satisfying times of my life. It was our initial sacrifice that helped the ministry look and feel like it feels today.

We were all trying to help Bishop promote the message. We knew the word was good; we just needed to help him get it to the masses. It didn't matter if we were doing two tapes or two hundred. We did it with the same spirit, a spirit of excellence. We never complained. We enjoyed doing it. It was fulfilling and we made it fun. When we look back on it today, we laugh. It is amazing how simple little things can turn into something so substantial.

As the ministry continued to grow, the demand began to exceed our expectations. Finally, in February of 1996, Bishop Jakes hired me as a full- time employee of the ministry. After seventeen years of working in the gas industry, I transformed from wearing jeans to wearing a business suit. I went from laying pipes to helping people. What a transformation! God had changed me from the inside, and now He was going to take me completely out of my comfort zone.

I remember one of my first major assignments as an employee of Temple of Faith; I worked the *"Man Power"* conference held in Cincinnati, Ohio. Gerald was the conference coordinator and Silas was the administrator at the time. Bishop told me to fly to Cincinnati so I could help Gerald and Silas out.

At the time I didn't think twice about it. I just packed my bags and headed to Cincinnati. I knew this was a very important luncheon. Bishop invited some of the local pastors to come out so we could get their support for the upcoming conference.

Once I got to Cincinnati, things began to register with me. This was totally different territory for me. I came from digging ditches to meeting with civic officials and local dignitaries in a matter of months. Now, it was essential for me to capitalize on my communication skills. I was dealing with pastors and preachers face to face and I didn't have any formal education to fall back on. All I could rely on was my upbringing. My parents always taught me to be a people person and I was. People never intimidated me. I was raised to be a confident young man. I have always been able to square my shoulders back and look people straight in the face. It didn't matter if they were the janitor or the CEO. I have always looked at people as just being people, no matter what their title or position was.

The next morning, I began to feel a level of expectancy in my spirit. I could not believe this phenomenal opportunity God had given me. I showered, brushed my teeth and got ready to go downstairs for the luncheon. As I got in the elevator, it was as if I could hear the old gospel tune, *"How I Made it Over,"* playing in my head. I started bobbing my head back and forth as I was listening to the beat in my head. This entire experience seemed too good to be true.

Then the Holy Spirit reminded me; once I joined Temple of Faith all I wanted to do was serve. Now, not only was I serving but also getting paid to do it. I found it ironic that the call of God on my life had made provision for me.

As much as I loved the Lord, I didn't have any idea He would operate like this. I enjoyed serving. I enjoyed making things happen and making sure things were in place. This is exactly what I had done in Cincinnati. As the elevator opened, it was symbolic of the door that was opening up in my life.
Right at that moment, the Holy Spirit spoke to me again and said, *"You are doing what I called you to do."*

I was so amused at how God turned my pain into His passion. I actually started laughing when I got off the elevator. There was a group of people waiting to get on. I am sure they thought I was weird because there wasn't anyone else on the elevator with me. They had no idea God had been talking to me the whole time I was riding down.

It was laughter that helped lighten my load that day. We worked maybe sixteen hours in total. First there was preparation, then presentation, and finally placement of the people. Overall, it was a very challenging day getting people in and out, but it was a tremendous blessing.

When I look back on it, it was all worth it. We did what we knew we had to do. We felt like we were helping a man fulfill a vision that was placed on his heart. Cincinnati was just the beginning for me. From that point on, we were busy, busy, and busy.

In one year, we probably held eight to ten conferences: *"Man Power"*, *"Woman, Thou Art Loosed"* and *"Back to the Bible"* to name a few. We would go from city to city. We were moving product, moving people and fulfilling the purpose.

As we continued to hold conferences, we developed a system until we got it down pat. We made it work and everybody contributed. There weren't any big I's or little you's. We joined forces and worked together as a tremendous team. We realized the bottom line was salvation. The more conferences we did, the more products we sold. Yet, the ultimate goal was to have people delivered and souls set free.

Although everyone worked in the background, we felt we were all helping to bring the ministry to the forefront. It was all about taking things to another level.

A lot of times people feel you have to be in the limelight to be blessed. Yet, the Word of God teaches us the blessings flow down. We were all following a great Man of God. His anointing was touching our lives in a way no one could imagine. We gave with our services and were ultimately blessed; yet God got the glory in the end.

* Scripture Reference

"Teach me thy way, O LORD, and lead me in a plain path, because of mine enemies."

Psalm 27:11 (KJV)

* Prayer

Lord, I ask You to be my guide as I tread on new soil. Allow my fears to decrease, as my faith increases. Let Your Word be my sword, and the Holy Spirit be a hedge of protection around me.

H.G.

CHAPTER TWELVE

Treading On New Territory: The Move To Dallas

"Faith is to believe what you do not see; the reward of this faith is to see what you believe."

~Saint Augustine

After a while, Denise and I began to get more involved with Temple of Faith. I was trying to adjust to my new role in full-time ministry. A few months before Bishop had hired me to work with his staff, he had gotten a call from a friend regarding a church that was being foreclosed in Dallas, Texas. It was almost the end of the year, and Bishop was focusing on what God told him to do next year. His friend told him there was a really nice piece of property in Dallas, and he could probably get a good deal on it. Even though we were bursting at the seams at Temple of Faith, I didn't think Bishop was really interested in the venture at the time.

A few months later, he received another call from his lawyer about the same building. I still didn't think it appealed to Bishop yet. Texas was really far away and it wasn't something he had given much thought to. Yet, his attorney friend was so convincing, it began to peak Bishop's curiosity.

The final word from his attorney was, *"You might want to fly down and at least look at it. If you don't see any interest, then I'll drop the issue completely."* Since this was the second call about the church, Bishop felt like it was something he needed to at least consider. After much thought and a lot of prayer, he agreed to look at the property.

Once he let us know he wanted to go to Dallas and take a look at the building, a weird feeling of anticipation came in the air. I knew Bishop would never make a move without consulting God first. None of us could have imagined what this trip would mean to the ministry. Bishop, along with his spiritual father, Dr. Watkins, a couple of other people and I headed to Dallas. We had one goal: to see this church everyone wanted Bishop to buy.

While on the plane, I literally had knots in my stomach. Every time the pilot hit an air pocket, my stomach jumped up into my chest. I wasn't sure if it was nervousness or excitement, but deep in my spirit I knew this trip was going to change my life in some way or another. I couldn't put my finger on it, but the pulse of this event was very different. In fact, we were all a little uneasy about what this trip might mean. Bishop was the quietest of us all. We knew he wanted nothing more than to hear from God.

Once we landed, our whirlwind trip began. We were greeted at the airport then taken straight to the church, which was located in the southern sector of Dallas. The church was called the Eagle's Nest. The owner was going through a financial crisis and having a hard time holding on to the facility. It was evident he was going to do everything to get rid of the property before it was foreclosed on.

When we pulled up to the church, chills went through my body. I had never seen anything like it before in my life. It was huge. I don't know about anyone else, but it was much larger than I anticipated. At first, it was hard for me to make my mind grasp what I was looking at. This facility was so much more than any of us had imagined.

Even though we were all excited, it was a contained excitement. Once I saw the building, I felt like a little boy standing outside a candy store waiting for a chance to go in. No one wanted to seem overzealous because we didn't know what God was going to say. As we walked through the building there was a sense of anticipation throughout all of us, but we tried to remain reserved.

We held on to our emotions because we knew the church was in trouble. We also knew we had an opportunity to venture out and obtain this larger building at a very good price.

Walking through the facility made me realize the limitless possibilities this place could represent. Yet, no matter what I felt inside, I was careful not to let anyone know my feelings. We kept conversations to a minimum between us. I knew Bishop needed to consult God before we took another step.

After we had a full tour of the building, Bishop separated himself from everyone. We all knew what that meant. He could already tell what we were thinking; now his attention had to turn to the Lord. He needed a serious word from Heaven before he could take this leap of faith.

We were so overwhelmed; we couldn't even contemplate what was going on in Bishop's mind. There were so many questions that needed to be answered, and so many decisions that needed to be made in such a short period of time. Ultimately, only God could answer these questions for him. I am sure Bishop knew whatever God said would impact the rest of his life.

As we wandered around the building, we all wanted to know what the Lord was saying. I knew he was listening with all his heart. Over the years, Bishop had demonstrated a strong and sincere ear to hear the voice of God, but this time, it had to be challenging. He had to know without a doubt what God was saying to him. There was so much at stake. Bishop knew wherever he was; his major commission was to bring people out of the darkness and into the light. God was using him to mold lives; now the question was where he would be most effective in doing it.

After we returned to West Virginia, it didn't take long for Bishop to announce he was going to purchase the property in Dallas. Although the purchase would take a lot of weight off the shoulder of the Pastor who owned it, this was about to put a tremendous burden on Bishop and our growing ministry.

Even though he was confident we were supposed to purchase the property, he was not fully convinced of the use of the building. He considered it being a convention center, conference hall in addition to being a church. The one thing we knew for sure was we were moving forward.

Once Bishop's decision was final, he called me into his office. He said, "*Holloway, I have a project for you to do. You went with me to Dallas, now I need you to go back to help prepare the facility for our move to Texas.*"

He pulled a piece of paper out of a drawer and began to jot some things down. He explained to me that he needed the color scheme of the church to be changed, additional pews to be added and an electrical upgrade. I listened and tried to make mental notes of what the building looked like during our initial visit. He began to dictate my new assignment.

When I left Bishop's office that afternoon, I didn't know how to feel. I knew there were other people who had worked with the ministry much longer than I. He could have easily given them the task. It was obvious this was going to be a huge responsibility. I didn't want to let Bishop down and I wanted to be successful in the call God placed on my life.

I have to admit, part of me felt so inadequate. I still had dirt under my fingernails from digging ditches. Now, I was going to be the forerunner for this next move of God in our church. I was about to face the first major challenge of my new position. I didn't have a handbook or manual to follow. There were no rules or anyone I could ask or consult with. I didn't have anyone else to look to for guidance. The main question in the back of my head was: what do you do when you don't know what to do? My only resolve was I had to **trust God when I couldn't trace Him.** I could not lean to my own understanding, because none of this made sense to me in the natural. I had to face the facts; this was a super natural situation and only God was going to be able to bring me through it.

After reviewing everything Bishop said about the possibilities in Dallas, my next step was to tell Denise. At the time, Denise had been with the telephone company for about twenty years. The transfer to Dallas could mean she would lose all her seniority and have to start from the ground floor again. To complicate the situation even more, she had recently lost her father. Here I was considering going to Texas, and she was still grieving.

Throughout our marriage, Denise had been my rock, my source of strength and my biggest supporter. However, when I went to her about moving to Dallas, I had no idea how she would respond.

Once again, her response superseded what I could imagine. She never thought twice about the situation. If she did, she did not let me know. Since we were in one accord, my next step was to prepare for the move to Texas.

My next trip to Dallas was going to be very different. This time there was not an entourage of people going; it was just me. There was no mystery about what the outcome of the trip would be. I was on a very distinct and detailed mission. I had three months to turn a vacant building into a worship center that would be indicative of a worldwide ministry. Our first trip was an exploratory venture. Now, we had purchased the property and Bishop had a plan. My sole objective was to make his plan a reality.

I was nervous on this trip but it was a different type of nervous. Many of my questions were answered but I still needed to be reassured God would be with me every step of the way. There is nothing like knowing your sole source is the Holy Spirit. I knew my success or failure was all contingent on my ability to walk in the path God planned for me.

When the plane landed in Dallas, there was a peace that came over me. Right then, the Lord dropped in my spirit, *"This is home."* All I could say was, *"Wow."* I didn't know anyone in Dallas. I didn't know where I was going and to be honest, I didn't even know what I was doing. However, this is how God works. If I could have done this in my own power, it would not have been the miraculous experience it was going to become.

When I think about it, I don't believe Bishop evaluated the assignment. He just knew what needed to be done and told me to do it. This is the way Bishop operates. He trusts God, and believes God will use people to get His work done.

Once I planted my feet on Dallas soil, I hit the ground running. There was so much to be done and so little time. As I headed to the church, I pulled out the list of contacts I had and I did not have one minute to waste. The next few months would be the most intense months of my life.

I worked six days a week. Most of the time I worked twelve to fourteen-hour days. The key to my success was to be able to multi-task. I had to hire contractors, electricians, painters, and construction workers. In my spare time, I found realtors to help look for housing for our executive team who would be relocating from West Virginia.

As I continued to work on the new facility, I realized when God gives you something bigger than you can handle, he always sends you angels to help fulfill the promise. The first angel I met was a guy named Thomas. Thomas was the maintenance man for the Eagle's Nest church. He knew the building like the backside of his hand. It was evident he knew what to do in about every situation that would arise.

Thomas was in a very vulnerable situation. Since we purchased the church, he was about to lose his job. Yet, his skills and resources were essential to what we needed. I knew Thomas could be a key player in making my task so much easier. I said to him, *"If you take care of me, I will take care of you. "* I knew he was very resourceful. He always knew what to do. He became a guide for me as I crossed off the items on my list of things to do. God strategically placed him there to teach me everything I needed to know about the Eagle's Nest.

After being in Dallas for about forty-five days, finally help was on the way. Bishop began to send other people down to assist me in bringing the vision into fruition. There were fifty families in all who made the transition from West Virginia to Dallas. Accounting, administration, finance and audio were the first areas to send people to assist with the new ministry.

Once the families arrived in Dallas, they were given about a month to find permanent housing.

With a little help from my friends, the ministry began to take shape. The work we were doing together was also indicative of the name Bishop had selected to call the new location. He was going to call it The Potter's House: A place of healing, hope and restoration. Within three months, we took an old foreclosed building and turned it into a plush five thousand-seat sanctuary.

Before the official launch of The Potter's House, everyone was here that was supposed to be. They were all ready to assist in the new vision. I could not believe my eyes. I was settled in a totally new environment and accomplished what Bishop had requested.

I think everyone connected with the ministry was overwhelmed with excitement. The atmosphere between us was electrifying. There was an underlying feeling knowing something was about to happen and it was going to blow our minds.

Once Denise arrived in Dallas, things became a little difficult. The ministry was coming together, but my family was falling apart. We were facing challenge after challenge in the transition. Denise didn't have a job. We weren't settled in a home yet, and our daughter Dana needed to get enrolled in school. We also didn't have any local family to assist us in this transition. Thank God for our church family. We had traveled a great distance, it was difficult, but we were determined to trust God.

Our house in West Virginia needed repairs when I left. My sister Priscilla looked after it when Denise came to Dallas. To our amazement, it sold in less than sixty days. This was almost unheard of. The house selling in record time was our sign we were on the right track, and God had our back.

Denise finally got a job with the local phone company. For a while it was a little frustrating for her because she had to start all over from the ground up. She was placed in an entry-level position. She hated even getting up and going to work. Deep inside, Denise knew our move to Dallas was God. I kept telling her the reward would be great if we stuck to the mission. I believed this was a test and it was essential for us to pass it.

Before long, the day that everyone was waiting for arrived. It was the first day of worship at The Potter's House. There are no words to describe the excitement we experienced the Sunday we opened the church doors. The entire city had anticipated this day. People drove from miles around just to take a look at the building. They heard about Bishop, they had seen him on television, and now they wanted the chance to see him in person. They could not believe he chose to move his ministry to Dallas. People knew the Lord was at work and celebrated with us.

By the end of service, everyone was on the edge of their seats. When Bishop finished preaching, he stretched his hands out, and said, *"Welcome to the Potter's House.*

Welcome Home!"

When he said those words it penetrated the atmosphere. His words melted the chains of people who were bound. People rushed to the altar from everywhere in the sanctuary. This wasn't even the altar call; this was a call for membership. As we watched the people rush forward, all of us connected with the ministry were baffled. Our minds were blown. This image superseded our expectations.

The altar was flooded with people wanting to join the church. There were fifteen hundred of them and only fifty of us. Needless to say, we were severely out numbered. We were literally pulling our hair out. The first question that needed to be answered was where in the world are we going to put all these people!

This first Sunday left us with our mouths hanging open. We had to regroup and redefine what our next steps would be. We had to come up with a plan of how to control what God had blessed us with. Handling the growth of The Potter's House was like a woman giving birth to a twelve-pound baby. No one knew how we were going to make this happen, but it had to happen.

After the first service, I stumbled to the back of the sanctuary. I took a seat in the last pew of the church. Looking around at how everything came together, it was remarkable. I was so overwhelmed; I cupped my head in my hands and began to cry. The Lord took me from digging ditches to walking in my destiny. I could see, even in the midst of my dilemmas, God had His hands on me. He was using a former drug addict to do a new thing in the Body of Christ. My three-month assignment was successfully completed. I stepped in to one of the greatest moves of God I had ever experienced. My task was finished, but my journey was about to begin.

* Scripture Reference

"For I know the plans I have for you, declares the LORD, plans for welfare and not for evil, to give you a future and a hope."

Jeremiah 29:11 KJV

Sometimes we are afraid of the next move because we are holding onto our last step. God is just waiting for us to trust Him for that next step, because it will change our life.

* Prayer

Lord, I know that my thoughts are not Your thoughts and my way is not Your ways. I realize that from the beginning of the earth You had me in mind. Now, I open myself up to marvel at what You have for me next. You have planted me in a soil where I can prosper. You have positioned me for success. As I press deeper into Your Word, I look forward to the tremendous things that will be revealed regarding this phase of my life.

H.G.

CHAPTER THIRTEEN

Next In Line For A Miracle

"For those who are willing to make an effort, great miracles and wonderful treasures are in store."

~Isaac Bashevis Singer

In the early 90's, I experienced a series of serious health issues. It all started when I was diagnosed with diabetes. None of my immediate family members were diabetic. Maybe I was the poster child for Type-Two Diabetes.

I was always thirsty and I began to lose weight quickly. In fact, I dropped almost twelve pounds within a three-week time span. I didn't know anything about diabetes, so I didn't realize these were all classic symptoms. Yet, these were enough signs to drive me to the doctor and find out what was going on with my body.

I was scared to go to the doctor. Part of the reason was because of my past drug use. When I was a junkie, my major concern was getting high; it wasn't medical hygiene. I was too concerned about getting my next hit. I used needles that weren't sterile all the time. The enemy put thoughts in my head that made me think I could be HIV Positive. With all these strange things happening in my body, my mind began to race. Of course the devil tormented me by saying, *"I got you."* However, in the middle of this emotional turmoil, the Lord gave me a word of peace. As clear as day, He spoke these words to me, *"I wouldn't clean you and leave your blood dirty. When I saved you, I cleansed you."*

This word from the Lord was like food to my soul. I desperately needed to hear it because the devil was playing tricks with my mind. I decided I was not going to give the enemy any space to dominate in my life. When I went in for my physical, I had the doctor test me for AIDS as well.

The test came back negative and it gave me all the ammunition I needed to shut up the enemy's voice. I didn't stop there; every year for the next seven years, I got tested for AIDS. The results were always negative.

* Losing My Sister *

I knew I didn't have time to be sick. The ministry was growing and my schedule was hectic. I was still trying to keep a pulse on my family in West Virginia. As the ministry grew, we were getting calls from everywhere. I remember getting the opportunity to visit Johannesburg, South Africa back in 1999. I was part of the team Bishop took with him.

I knew this was an opportunity of a lifetime. We only had about five days left on the trip and everyone was shopping for souvenirs, but my heart was a little heavy. I could not get my sister Rena off my mind. Before I left the country, I stopped to visit her in West Virginia. Rena was a diabetic. She was also losing her eyesight. Even though I knew her condition wasn't the best, I took the opportunity to encourage her. I loved her dearly and I wanted her to hold on to hope.

Rena was like a light in the community. She had a heart of gold. Whenever I came to visit, she would always have kids running in and out of her home. I could not believe all the activity. They would be playing games, eating or watching TV. Even though she only had two sons, she could have easily been considered the block mother. Her philosophy was, the more kids, the merrier. The last time I saw her, I could tell she was tired and she was weak.

Now, here I was in the middle of this small group trying to enjoy our shopping excursion. Bishop joined us after a while. All of a sudden, my phone rang. I hadn't gotten many calls, so I knew this was important.

When I got the phone to my ear, the voices on the other end were familiar. It was my mother and my oldest sister, Priscilla. Once I heard their voices, I became anxious; I knew something was up.

Priscilla blurted out, *"We have got to make a decision."*
Trying to keep my mind from racing, I said, *"About what?"* By
this time my mother chimed in, *"Rena is not doing good. She
is on a respirator."*

After hearing my mother's comment, I let out a deep sigh. I
knew this was not going to be an easy call. They went on to
tell me we could leave her on the respirator, or we could take
her off to see if she could make it on her own.

In my heart, I knew this would be a difficult decision but there
was only one answer. I knew how active Rena was and there
was no way she would want to live on a respirator. To break
the tension, I said, *"Listen, ya'll know Rena just as well as I do.
Rena wouldn't want to live like that. Let's take her off the
respirator. If she lives, it is God's will. If she doesn't live, we
have to trust God."*

By the time I hung up the phone, my mother and Priscilla had
agreed with my response. They knew we had to honor my
sister's lifestyle. We couldn't just keep her hanging on to keep

ourselves happy. We had to release her and allow God to do the rest.

After I hung up the phone, I began to think about the last time I saw Rena. I could still see a very vivid picture of Rena in my mind and she looked so exhausted. I knew it wouldn't be fair to her to just keep holding on like that.

I loved my sister so much but I knew the decision we made might mean that Rena wouldn't be with us much longer. My heart was broken at the thought of losing one of my siblings. I began to weep.

I was crying so hard I lost track of everything that was going on around me. I didn't even notice when Bishop got in the van. I think someone must have missed me and told him I was in the van. I am sure everyone noticed the concerned look on my face when I answered the phone.

Whatever the reason was, Bishop showed up at the right time. I had a chance to explain to him what was going on with

Rena. As I gave him the scenario, I broke down and started crying all over again. Unlike any one I know, he always had the right words to say at the right time. In this time of crisis, Bishop was there as my pastor but also a long time friend.

I know the situation had him a little chocked up as well. He said, *"We got you, Holloway. You don't have to wait for the next few days. We will get you out of here right now so you can go home to your family."*

Before I even had time to focus on it, the arrangements were made. I returned to the United States to say farewell to Rena. There is no way to express how difficult it is to say good-bye to a sibling. Rena and I had always been very close. She was only two years older than I. This didn't seem fair that diabetes had claimed her life so young.

* My Health Challenges *

After Rena died, I began to have my own health challenges. For years the enemy tried to consume me with something that was not real by taunting me with AIDS. Yet, my biggest challenge would come when I had to deal with something that was very real. After a while, my diabetes was coupled with a disease that was prominent in my family, hypertension. Hypertension, commonly known as high blood pressure, became my new foe. Over the years, the combination of my past drug use, diabetes, and hypertension began to work on my kidneys.

Over time, doctors began to monitor my kidneys. Their ability to function on their own was decreasing. By the year 2000, I only had thirty percent usage of my kidneys. When kidney usage decreases to lower than seventy five percent, it is considered Chronic Renal Failure. A year later, my kidneys were only working at fifteen percent. At this point, the doctors felt I was a prime candidate for dialysis. Dialysis was my only option for survival. Even though I was in the hospital, I thought this decision was rash. The idea of dialysis caught me off guard. The doctors wanted me to make a decision right away, and I refused to do it.

I just could not imagine them putting a shunt in my arm and hooking me up to a machine just to purify my blood. I had never done this, and I didn't want to deal with it. No matter how hard they tried to convince me, I was bull headed. I would not budge. Since, I wouldn't bend, my wife called Bishop.

Before I knew it, Bishop was paying me a visit in the hospital. He had a level of persuasion that no one else had over me. He had known me almost as long as my parents. He also lost his father to chronic renal failure when he was a teenager. He wasn't about to allow me to go down the same road.

When all was said and done, I agreed to go ahead with dialysis. They put the shunt in my arm to prepare me for the process. The cruel reality was, I had to realize my life expectancy would dwindle severely without dialysis. Kidneys help cleanse the blood. If I did absolutely nothing, I would be setting myself up for an infection and all kinds of other diseases. Even though I didn't want to do dialysis, I found out people easily lived twenty years or more by doing this treatment.

Before long, dialysis became a part of my regular routine for the next three and half years. Every other day, Monday, Wednesday and Friday, I went for treatment like clockwork. I knew this process would save my life and I had to make it work. The hospital also set me up with a social worker to help facilitate the procedure.

Though I had been a junkie for over sixteen years, the thing I liked the least about dialysis was being stuck in the arm. It was ironic. I had shot cocaine and heroin in the same vein they put my shunt in for years. I didn't think about it when I was doing drugs, but this time having that needle placed in my arm was painful. It was amazing, the same vein I was using to take my life by doing drugs, was now giving me life.

During my dialysis treatments, they would give me numbing cream to help take some of the pain away. Besides managing that, my treatments went seamlessly.

Occasionally, I would have too much fluid from over the weekends. This would cause me to cramp a little bit. I particularly remember once when I was on the road; I had taken in quite a bit of fluid over the weekend. My legs and arms began to cramp so bad I had to be admitted to the hospital. I said to God, *"I can't be sick like this and do what You called me to do."* Even though this wasn't a prayer, the moment I mumbled those words something changed.

After I recovered from that situation, I learned to gauge my fluid and watch my water intake. At first, it seemed like I was mastering the illness, but after a while the kidney sickness became challenging. Yet, once I vocalized my concern, I heard God's response: *"I got you."* Once the Word reached my spirit, it clicked like a key unlocking a door. I no longer focused on my dialysis regimen; I put the entire situation into God's very capable hands.

H.G.

Throughout my treatment, I continued to travel with Bishop Jakes across the country and I continued to serve. Sometimes my schedule was relentless. For instance, there were times we would get into Los Angeles on Sunday night. I would get up at 3:00 am on Monday morning. I would get dialysis from 5:00 AM until 9:00 AM. Next, I would prepare for whatever was on Bishop's agenda for the day. It could be anything from a book signing to a book tour, from a radio or television interview to preaching or holding a mid-week bible study. Sometimes it was all of the above. No matter what, I was prepared for whatever the day had to offer.

We could start a week in Los Angeles, then be in in Denver by Wednesday and in Seattle by Friday. Wherever we were, my social worker would have already made arrangements for me to receive dialysis in that city.

As I continued to travel, it was difficult, but I could not allow my condition to affect me. I knew I had a call on my life and I wanted to fulfill it. I felt that if I let my sickness get to me, I would not be able to fulfill my call. Therefore, when I left the hospitals, my days were just beginning.

People thought it was odd when I went back to work after finishing dialysis, but I had a job to do. I told God I wanted to fulfill what He placed in my hands to do, and I did. It was the Lord who helped me do my job effectively everyday, and I am thankful for that.

While receiving dialysis, I met another patient who had been receiving dialysis for twenty years. Seeing him reminded me that the process could go on for a while. My social worker told me, on an average, people waited two to three years before they would receive a kidney.

In the United States more than four thousand people die each year while they are waiting for a kidney. Unfortunately, many African Americans become too sick before they find a suitable match. I didn't want to become another statistic. I wanted to give myself every possible chance to find a suitable kidney donor, so I had my social worker place my name on every possible list domestically and internationally. From the very beginning, I had my mind made up that I was going to do what I had to do, and keep it moving.

* Michael Dies *

It seemed like once I got into a rhythm with receiving dialysis, something else came my way. One morning I was sitting at my desk at work and I received a phone call from my sister, Priscilla. She never called me at work, so I figured something might be wrong. The moment I heard the squeakiness in her voice, I froze. It was obvious something had happened. As I listened to her, I tried to prepare myself for what she was going to say next.

"What's going on?" I asked, hoping to get her to get straight to the point. Yet, my question was only greeted with silence. Weeping followed the silence. I was afraid to ask any more questions. I knew Priscilla was a strong woman. If whatever

was going on was enough to make her cry, then it had to be serious. One last time, I asked, *"What is wrong?"*

She said, *"Michael's dead."*

"Michael's what?"

"Michael had a heart attack this morning, and he is dead."

"You have got to be kidding me, Priscilla. Michael can't be dead."

"Holloway, I wish that I was kidding. Michael is really dead."

"Okay, let me call Denise. I'll call you back as soon as I find out when we can get home."

Still crying, Priscilla said, *"Okay."* Then she hung up the phone.

I was still holding on to the receiver as I began to wail like a baby. I could not believe this. My sister was dead; now my only brother was dead too? This just could not be. This was so unexpected. I had just spoken to him a few days before. His death caught me completely off guard.

Before I knew it, I was surrounded by my co-workers. The word of Michael's death had traveled down the corridors of our offices of the church. Gerald, Beverly, and Pastor Robinson came into my office to give their support. They were all from West Virginia and knew my family.

Gerald was the Administrator of the Potter's House. He did not hesitate to tell me to get my things and go home. He knew I was in no condition to work the rest of the day. As I started to leave the office, they let me know they would be making arrangements to come to Charleston for the services.

I left the office by about 3:00 PM. Driving down Interstate 20 was more difficult than normal. Even though I could manage the traffic, I could not stop the tears from rolling down my checks. Although I tried to keep my eyes focused on the road, I could not stop thinking about my brother. Michael was only fifty years old. I could not believe he was dead.

At home, my wife Denise had already started making arrangements for us to leave Dallas. Michael's death was a devastating blow for both of us. She knew one of us had to try to keep it together. It was important for us to remain strong, at least for the sake of my mother and my sister.

At first I was walking through the house aimlessly. Then I began putting a few things in my luggage. After a while, I began telling Denise and our daughter, Dana, how we were going to handle our travel arrangements to Charleston.

As I continued to pack my bags, the telephone rang. When I answered the phone, the voice on the other end asked, *"Is this Holloway Gray?"*

Wondering who in the world could be calling me right now, I responded, *"Yes, this is Holloway."*

Once the person on the other end confirmed who I was, she said, *"This is Methodist Hospital. I am calling to let you know we have a kidney for you. I just need to know how soon you can get here."*

Holding onto the receiver, I sat down on the bed. I looked out into the room with a blank stare. I am not sure how long it took me to answer her, but I knew it took a few minutes. After

I got my composure together, I said, *"Ma'am I really appreciate it, but I can't come."*

This was definitely not the response she expected. It took three years for me to get in this position. I should have been leaping up and down for joy. I should have been jumping around like a kid on a playground. Instead, I was almost despondent. The nurse was dumbfounded by my response. She said, *"Excuse me?"*

I said, *"Ma'am, I am sorry. I can't come."*

"Why?" she asked.

"My only brother just died of a heart attack this morning. If I take this kidney, I am not going to be able to help my family bury my brother. I can't do that."

"Mr. Gray, I will have the doctor call you back."

"Okay, that's fine."

By the time I hung up the phone, Denise was standing right by me. She had been hanging on to my every word.

"What are you doing, Holloway? You have to take this kidney," she said waving her hands in the air.

She was frustrated and she was frantic. There was no way she wanted me to pass up this opportunity.

"You have to do this Holloway. This is what you have been waiting for," she implored.

Denise was determined she could convince me to change my mind. Yet, there was something stronger than words. It was my commitment to my family. My father was dead, my sister was dead, and now my only brother was dead. I would have to be the man to step up to the plate for my mother and my only surviving sister, Priscilla. I owed that much to my family.

"Baby, I can't do this. They are not going to allow me to travel once I get the kidney. I know they won't hold my brother out long enough for me to recover and get to West Virginia."

There was no reasoning with Denise about this. She was livid over my decision. As she continued to try to reason with me, the phone rang again. This time it was the doctor.

"Is this Mr. Gray?"

"Yes, ma'am it is."

"They told me you wouldn't take the kidney we have offered you."

"Yes, ma'am, that is correct. You have to understand my brother just died today of a heart attack. We have to make funeral arrangements for him. We just started pulling the family together. I wouldn't feel right receiving life for myself, and not being there to bury my brother."

There was a long pause on the other end of the phone. The doctor said, *"Normally, we don't do this."*

Then she added, *"I understand what you are doing. I am not going to remove your name off the donor list. When you turn down an organ, you go to the bottom of the list. But, you go home and help your family bury your brother. We won't remove you from the list. We will keep you right where you are."*

I couldn't believe my ears. *"I really appreciate it. I am very grateful and thankful."* I was overcome by her generosity and kindness. She said, *"You do what you have to do for your family,"* as she hung up the phone.

Denise and I went home to bury Michael. I comforted my family and they comforted me. Once again, we were dealing with a lost which seemed almost unbearable. As we all said our final goodbyes, I was so glad God allowed me to have this last tribute to Michael. He had always been there for me when I was coming up; I don't think I could have lived knowing I was not there for him one final time.

After I got back to work, things were really busy. The Potter's House was preparing for its first *Mega* Conference in Atlanta. For years, Bishop Jakes hosted the *"Woman, Thou Art Loosed"* conference and The *"Man Power"* conference at separate times. This conference was not just *"Woman, Thou Art Loosed"*, but it was *"Man Power"* and a children's experience as well. It was three conferences in one. We didn't know what to expect, we had never done anything like this before.

Some of the top gospel artists were going to be at the Georgia Dome to kick this event off. Joyce Meyers, Juanita Bynam, Noel Jones, Creflo Dollar, and Paula White were some of the speakers. This was the biggest conference we have ever done. We named this event, *"MegaFest."* Churches and media outlets were talking about this all over the country. There was so much anticipation about it; we were all on the edge of our seats.

It was hard to believe that less than a month after Michael's death, Denise and I were headed to Atlanta for *"MegaFest"*. We didn't often get to travel together, so this was a wonderful opportunity. Even though we didn't get to see each other much, it was great to still be at a conference together. The conference exceeded all of our expectations. There was a record-breaking crowd of over 80,000 people in attendance for the event.

After *"MegaFest"* was over, Denise and I went back to our hotel room preparing to return to Dallas. Then the phone rang.
"Is this Holloway Gray"
"Yes, it is."

"This is Methodist Hospital in Dallas, Texas. We have a possible kidney for you."

"Really?"

"Yes, when can you be here?"

I began to explain I was in Atlanta, but I would make sure I was on the next plane to Dallas. The nurse began to give me very detailed instructions about what to do when I arrived in Dallas.

On the flight back home, Denise and I were so excited. We could not believe I was getting a second chance this soon. The conference had been so successful, and it was being topped off by this wonderful opportunity. This was outstanding.

When we arrived in Dallas, we went straight to Methodist Hospital. It felt like a big maze as we maneuvered through the halls. I was nervous, excited, and scared all at the same time. We finally found our way and met up with the doctors. Once we got there, they told us all the details. There was a lady from Puerto Rico who was the number one candidate for the kidney. I was the backup person.

When the doctors explained it to me I asked, *"What does this mean?"* The doctor said, *"Well, she is actually the person who is the recipient of the kidney. If by chance her immune system is not strong enough or something happens to her body where she is unable to receive the kidney, then you are next in line to receive it."*

I know for some people it may not have been the perfect solution, but for me it was great. I was excited, and Denise and I were extremely happy.
I looked at the doctor and shook his hand. I said, *"That's fine."*

The doctor directed Denise and I to a hospital room. He said, *"We will just have you stand by until we find out."*
Once Denise and I settled in the hospital room, we joined hands and began praying for the woman from Puerto Rico. We didn't know what was going on with her, but we knew she

needed this kidney as well. We asked God to prepare her immune system to receive the kidney and strengthen her body. We began to petition heaven for this woman whom we'd never even met.

After we prayed, we waited in the room for about two hours. The doctor returned to give us the news. The lady's immune system was not strong enough; they were going to have to prepare me for surgery. Denise and I looked at each other. I just sighed, and said, *"Wow."* I could not believe this.

By this time, it was late in the evening: about 8:00 pm. They were preparing me for surgery in the next hour. The doctor began to explain what was going to happen. In the midst of his conversation, instead of saying I was going to receive one kidney, he said *"kidneys."*

My wife was just as stunned and baffled as I was. This entire time, we only thought I needed one kidney. I wasn't sure if I understood the doctor correctly or not.
"What do you mean kidneys?" I asked.

The doctor said, "*The donor was a two-year-old baby. We are going to give you both of the kidneys.*"
Words could not come to my mind. All I could say, once again, was, "*Wow!*"

Denise and I were blown away by this news. We had never heard that they could do a transplant from a baby to an adult. With a puzzled look on her face, Denise asked, "*Is that possible?*"
The doctor smiled and said, "*Yes, we do it all the time.*"

Once the doctor left the room, Denise and I started acting like a couple of school kids. We grabbed each other's hands and started swinging them in the air. We were rejoicing, praising God, and celebrating all at the same time. In my heart, I was singing, "Look what the Lord has done."

A few minutes later, the nurse came in and prepared me for the surgery. By 9:30 PM they had taken me into the operating room. The surgery lasted almost two hours.

When it was over, I was in a lot of pain. They sedated me so I felt better. I was no longer in severe pain, but I could still feel the discomfort. Yet, the pain really didn't matter. I was just grateful that I had another opportunity at life. I could not believe God had been so gracious me. Now, I had a new birthday, June 22, 2005.

Although I listened to the doctors, I still had no idea what to expect. So, I set an unrealistic expectation for my recovery. I felt like after I got the transplant, I would be back on my feet in about six months.

To my surprise, it took eighteen months for me to feel normal again. My new kidneys didn't adapt to my body as well as they were supposed to. We had several challenges after my surgery. As my kidneys tried to adjust to their new home, I was in and out of the hospital quite frequently.

I normally weighed about two hundred ten pounds; I ended up losing about sixty-five pounds while my body recovered from the transplant. I even went through a phase of depression and anxiety because this was not what I expected.

As I struggled to get back to normal, I began to experience feelings of emptiness and loneliness. Denise was by my side the entire time, but there were still some things she couldn't feel for me. My internal journey had to be completed alone. I think some of my emotions may have been driven by the medications I was taking.

When it came down to the external healing process, Denise was there for me every step of the way. She was preparing my food and medications in the morning and praying with me at night.

Denise was more than a helpmeet. Her response and support were overwhelming to me. What she did for me, this time, I was not able to do for myself. She was exceptional in her support for me until I got back on my feet.

On several occasions, it felt like my body was going to reject the kidneys. The rejection process was almost like the side effects of chemotherapy. I had severe soreness and pain. Still, I rejoiced in everything. I celebrated the soreness as well as the pain. All of it gave me joy.

I knew God blessed me with these kidneys in spite of what I was going through. Every time I went to the hospital, I had to remind myself that I was blessed. All I could think was, *"Surely, God wouldn't give me these kidneys to take them back."*

The devil tried to play with my mind every time I had a setback. He made me feel like this was it; the battle was over. Deep inside, I knew I had the victory. Just knowing I had a second chance at life was the greatest reward I could experience.

I believe because of my faithfulness in serving God, not man, I was blessed beyond compare. I turned down one kidney in order to bury my brother. Now, I was blessed with two kidneys from a two-year-old child. They were not abused or misused. I could not have asked for a better scenario.

As I reflect on this miraculous experience in my life, I attribute God's faithfulness to me from my obedience to Him. Once again, God gave me life. Now I was giving myself back to Him through my service and dedication to the kingdom.

* Scripture Reference

"Remember Lot's wife. [33] Whosoever shall seek to save his life shall lose it; and whosoever shall lose his life shall preserve it."

Luke 17: 32-33 (KJV)

* Prayer

Lord, don't let me hold onto anything as though it is more valuable that the purpose You have for my life. Let me always be willing to set myself aside so that I can embrace You.

CHAPTER FOURTEEN

Getting Off Course: Jody Dies

"There are things we don't want to happen but have to accept, things we don't want to know but have to learn, and people we can't live without but have to let go."

~Proverb

The year after my kidney transplant, things were back to normal. Before I knew it, I was planning for *"MegaFest"* once again. I landed in Atlanta for The Potter's House 2005 *"MegaFest"* Conference. There was so much excitement in the air. Last year's conference had broken the Georgia Dome's record for attendance with over 140,000 people turning out for one night's service. We had no idea what to expect this year. Preparations were made for at least 500,000 people to attend this four-day event.

As I rushed through Atlanta's Hartsfield Airport, my cell phone rang. I quickly grabbed it, realizing it could be anyone, from Bishop Jakes to one of our administrative support team members who were still in Dallas.

To my surprise, it was my sister's youngest son, Drake. I could barely understand him because he was crying so hard.
His call caught me off guard. I tried to get him to calm down so I could at least understand what he was saying. I said, *"Drake, what's wrong?"*

Still crying uncontrollably, he said, *"Uncle Holloway, I think Jody has been shot. "*

There was so much noise in the airport I really couldn't hear him so I responded, *"Do what?"*
Even though I couldn't tell what was going on, I knew it was ripping him apart. Little did I know, I was about to share in Drake's pain.

Then as clear as day, I heard him yell, *"Jody got shot!"*

I stopped in the middle of my tracks, as I headed to the baggage claim area. I held on to the phone as I gasped for my breath. *"What happened?"* I asked anxiously.

Choking on his words, Drake responded, *"I don't know."*

At that moment, the father in me kicked in because it was not enough information. I could not act on this because I needed more details.

The first thing I had to do was get Drake to calm down. *"Drake, I need you to find out what happened,"* I said, trying to keep my composure.

Then I added, *"I will come home if I need to. I need for you to find out what happened so you can tell me what is going on. Then call me back."*

As I hung up the phone, numbness came over my body. In an instant, I went from rushing through the airport to just waiting. I didn't know whether to grab my bags or book a flight to

Charleston. For a moment, my body was so disjointed, I thought I was going to faint. I sat down in the nearest chair as I tried to pull myself together.

Rubbing my head, I tried to process the information I had just been given. I wondered how in the world I was going to tell Denise. Then the phone rang. It was Denise, someone had already gotten to her with the news.

As she began to shriek on the phone, I knew I was going to have to be the strong one. I said, *"Honey, we don't know. Don't panic. We will find out what happened,"* trying to reassure her everything was going to be okay. Yet, there was nobody there to reassure me.

I just wanted her to relax because I was so far away from her. I couldn't look into her warm brown eyes; I couldn't hold her and I couldn't protect her. All I could do was give her a few words through a plastic phone and pray they would suffice until we knew something else.

H.G.

Before she hung up, I said, *"It might just be someone saying something. We don't know that it is true. Drake is going to call me back."*

Waiting on Drake's call was like waiting on the next shoe to drop. It took an eternity, but his call would reveal the one thing I did not want to know. My son had been shot, but Drake did not know if he was alive or dead.

Now, my next move was already planned; I had to go home. After I spoke to my wife, I called Bishop to tell him I was going to have to leave. He was still in California preparing to come to Atlanta for the conference. When he heard the tension in my voice, he asked, *"What's going on?"* Not wanting to break down in the airport, I just said, *"Jody has been shot, and they think he might be dead."*

After I gave him the news, there was a pause on the phone. I know it was only a few seconds, but it seemed like almost five minutes. Then he began to bombard me with questions. I responded, *"I really don't know Bishop, I just need to go."*

Before I could even finish my sentence, he said, *"You go ahead to Charleston and I will meet you there."*

I knew this conference was going to be huge, and he did not need to be distracted by this. I didn't even know how much of it was true. Sometimes people will tell you a lie just to get you stirred up. From past experiences, I knew this could go from *"Jody's been shot"* to *"Jody was somewhere where there was shooting going on"*. I also knew, even if he was shot this did not have to be life threatening.

I said, *"Bishop, this might not be true: don't come. I will call you later,"* trying to convince him that everything was going to be okay. As I hung up the phone, Bishop's last words were, *"I will be there."*

Grabbing my bags from in front of the carousel, I called Beverly, Bishop's Executive Assistant, who worked close to me in the executive department; she was also a friend. Without going into a lot of details, I explained to her what happened and said that I would need to get on the next flight to Charleston.

After I hung up the phone, something in my chest dropped; I knew it had to be my heart. The blood was rushing so fast through my veins; it felt like my skin was going to be ripped wide open. I felt dizzy, nauseous, and sick all at the same time. All I could think was, this had to be a bad dream.

When I'd first arrived at Atlanta's Hartsfield Airport, my mind was rushing with what was next on the agenda for "MegaFest". Now, I was just contemplating if I would ever look into my son's eyes again.

After Beverly called me back with the details for my new flight, I rechecked my bags for my flight to Charleston and I headed to the boarding gate. Atlanta has one of the busiest airports in the world. It is amazing how you can be around thousands of people and still feel lonely.

There was a deep darkness that began to creep into my soul as I tried to find out what gate I was flying out of. When I got to the gate, I took a seat far from everyone else. I just needed to be by myself. I tried to hold on to my emotions, but once I sat down the tears began to flow. I put my head between my hands and I called on God with everything in me. I begged and pleaded with Him not to let any of this be true. Like a gambler, I was trying to make a deal with God. I was willing to accept anything; I just didn't want Jody to be dead.

I was so caught up; I almost didn't hear it when my flight was called. I just happened to notice everyone heading toward the aircraft door. I grabbed my carry-on bag and headed to the back of plane. Fortunately, it was not a full flight. I was able to sit in the back near a window all by myself. The entire time I was on the aircraft, I was praying.

Even though the flight was a little over an hour, it seemed like a lifetime. I started thinking back to when Denise and I were in high school and she told me she was pregnant with Jody. The first thing I asked her to do was get her things and get out of my locker. I wasn't even eighteen years old; I had no concept of fatherhood.

Denise and her mother clearly let me know Jody was going to be born no matter what I decided to do. They were both strong, praying women. Their prayers were strong enough to overcome my objections; maybe they would be strong enough to overcome this situation as well.

When I got to Charleston, it was a little after10:00 PM. I was physically drained, spiritually suppressed, and emotionally stressed. Still, I rented a car and headed straight to Jody's apartment. Riding down Daniel Boone Drive to the Washington Manor Projects was such a familiar route for me. This was the same place where I grew up.

As I pulled up to the brick buildings, I felt emptiness inside me. These buildings that kept me as a little boy, were betraying me as a man. I had played on their steps, walked in their hallways, and now my own son's blood was captured in their corridors.

Looking at the trash on the ground and a few taped up windows, I knew this place had changed. This was no longer the clean, community-oriented place I'd been so proud of as a child.

There were people who migrated to the city from Detroit and New York. Many of them were living in Washington Manor. The buildings had become known for criminal activity. It was no longer a safe place to live. Shootings had become common and gang life had become the norm.

Standing in front of Jody's apartment gave me an eerie feeling. Yet, there were no telltale signs of what happened. No yellow tape outside, no white chalk marking, nothing to indicate the answer to the one question in my mind. Was my son still alive?

My next stop would be the Charleston Police Department. Although I experienced run-ins with the law when I was growing up, this visit would be different. This time I was not approaching the police department as a suspect, but as the father of a victim. Police buildings always had such a cold feeling to them. They lacked emotion and feeling and sometimes, information.

As I walked in and asked an officer one the hardest questions of my life, his response took my breath away. He answered the one question that plagued my soul. He confirmed that Jody was dead.

They didn't give me a lot of information because the incident had just happened. Once the news was confirmed, I staggered out of the police station like a drunken man onto the streets of Charleston. I came to the city still holding on to hope; now all hope was gone. Now all I could do was hold on to God.

As the tears began to roll down my face, I heard one word from the Lord, it was, *"Live."* I had no idea what to live for, but in the midst of death, God was telling me to live. That one word would become the anchor for my soul. Every time I cried out to God for help, His word kept holding me together, especially when I thought I would fall apart.

By the time I got in the car and left the police station, my cell phone rang. It was Bishop; he had just landed in Charleston. If I needed a pastor or a friend, this would be the time. He'd made the detour from California to Charleston, but he had three guests with him. They were all heading to "MegaFest" with Bishop, but he made a detour to help his brother out in a crisis.

Once they arrived, I booked them rooms at a hotel. After everyone checked in, we all went up to Bishop's room. When I looked into Bishop's eyes, my head fell down onto his chest; I had no idea how bad off I was. I had spent the last few hours trying to be strong. Now, in the company of friends, I had to admit I was weak.

For a few minutes, no one said a word; my tears just began to flow. Finally, I tried to pull myself together. I couldn't understand why I had not fallen to the floor. Then I looked, and they were all embracing me with one of the most powerful group hugs imaginable.

Just like an old friend, Bishop gave me comforting words. Like a pastor he spoke into my sprit. Like a master facilitator, he began to arrange every aspect of Jody's funeral. From the flowers to the funeral home, he took care of everything.

That night, my pastor, my friend and my comrade all became one. He ministered to me with Biblical words of wisdom. He comforted me as we reflected on Jody's childhood antics. He consoled me by reminding me I had to be strong. Life would go on, even in the midst of tragedy.

Like a good shepherd, he began to whirl questions in the air like *"what do you need, what do you want, and what can we do for you?"* In a split second, he went from being my pastor to someone who was serving me. I could not believe I had begged him not to come, but I was so thankful and grateful he was there. There was no way I could have made it without his support.

At this point, my life was in shambles and I was in complete shock. I didn't have a clue what to do next. I knew I had just experienced every parent's nightmare. I had lost a child. I didn't know why. I didn't know who and I didn't even know exactly when. The one thing I did know: my heart was broken.

Even though *"MegaFest"* was about to start, Bishop stayed for a day and a half. By the time he left for Atlanta, everything was done, from the obituary to the finalization of the funeral service. My only major task was to get my family from Dallas back to Charleston.

When Bishop left for *"MegaFest"* everything seemed so final. After twenty-nine years, Jody was about to be laid to rest. In the next week, Bishop Jakes would make one more trip back to Charleston; it would be to eulogize my son.

Bishop and his wife, Serita, were a tremendous blessing to our entire family. They manifested the love of God as they comforted my family during our darkest hour.

Their unconditional love helped sustain us. It got us through our hard situation, but the pain was still there. Nothing could fill the void of losing my only son. When I picked up the phone to dial his number, no one was there to answer. One of the most valuable pieces of my life was gone. For years my family would try to piece things back together. However, our efforts would be like mending shattered glass.

Losing Jody was one of the most valuable lessons of my life. I learned to lean on God when I had no clue what to do next. We weathered the storm, but it was not without a price. It took two and a half years of Christian counseling to help us master this crisis. This was just a portion of the cost we had to bear. We tried to put our lives back together with one piece missing. God gave us grace when the lights went out in our lives. There is no doubt in my mind that having God on our side made the biggest difference. For years, our emotions swung back and forth like a pendulum. We were confused, we were angry, and we were frustrated.

In many ways, Jody's death was still a mystery. There were still so many unanswered questions. From what we could piece together, someone broke in with the intent to rob him. When he arrived home that night, the robbery turned into a murder. He died from a gunshot wound to the head. In order to solve the mystery, we personally offered a 10,000 dollar reward for any leads that would bring closure to the case. Even still, there were no calls, no inquiries, absolutely nothing.

The lack of response only confirmed one thing to me, the community had changed. It was no longer a place where people cared about each other; it was now a gang-infested environment and everyone was afraid to talk.

There was one person who was held as a suspect for Jody's death, but the prosecutors had to release him because there was not enough evidence to detain him. Later, the same man would be convicted for killing someone else.

For years, all we wanted were answers, but we couldn't get answers. The counseling helped us to at least get back to where we are today. We are still not where we should be, but at least we have found some form of peace with the situation.

No parent expects to bury his or her child. When the order is reversed there is an insurmountable void. However, In the midst of my private storm, God calmed my soul. Through the eyes of the Lord, I began to look at the situation from a different prospective. Instead of saying, "why did this happen?" God reminded me, Jody wasn't mine anyway. He was just on loan to my wife and I; he always belonged to God.

Once the Lord gave me that revelation, it changed my entire disposition. I began to thank God for the twenty-nine years we had with Jody. I went from sorrow to gratitude. I thanked God for the relationship, the love and everything we experienced together.

Not only was my son just like me, he was me. He was the part of me that no one could ever take away. I realized God didn't have to allow me to have a son. For this, I was truly grateful.

H.G.

Reflecting on our relationship, I recalled when I was growing up giving my mother a lot of trouble. She warned me, "Just wait until you have children of your own." Well, Jody was mine and I experienced it all with him.

We had good times and we had bad times, but I would not change anything. He loved us for who we were, and we loved him for who he was. Even though he was gone, he will always live within our hearts.

* Scripture Reference

"Be anxious for nothing, but in everything by prayer and supplication, with thanksgiving, let your requests be made known to God; [7] and the peace of God, which surpasses all understanding, will guard your hearts and minds through Christ Jesus."

Philippians 4:6-8 (KJV)

* Prayer

Lord, as storms of life are all around me, give me peace. Allow me not to lean on my understanding, but let me face my trials with the mind of Christ and the heart of the Holy Spirit.

CHAPTER FIFTEEN

Trusting God When You Can't Trace Him

"He who breathes into our hearts the heavenly hope, will not deceive or fail us when we press forward to its realization. "

~ Albert Benjamin Simpson

(From the book "Days of Heaven Upon Earth")

It took a long time for us to get over Jody's death. Still to this day, there is a part of him that lives on deep inside my soul. However, Jody's death would not be the last major challenge for me.

There comes a time in life when you are pushed to the very limit, and you can only contemplate where the breaking point might be. It is here where our faith gets challenged and we have to rely on the anchor we have in Christ. His faithfulness always proves to us, when we are at the end of our rope, God always has an extension cord.

At the beginning of 2012, I found myself facing one challenge after another. As soon as I got over one hurdle, there was another one staring me in the face. It wasn't like I couldn't adjust to adversity or handle hardship, but this time things were coming faster than I could keep up with. Some of the challenges I had to face with my health were old, but they had a new twist to them.

It all started in such a simple way. I was hungry. I went through the drive thru of a fast food restaurant to grab a quick bite to eat. This wasn't a restaurant I normally frequented, but it was close to home and I wanted something in a hurry. I got a burger and some onion rings and headed home. I could barely get the wrapper off the food before I chomped down on it. I must have taken a couple of bites and the food was gone, I was so famished.

By the next morning, I realized I'd made a bad choice in my food selection. It felt like my stomach was doing somersaults all night long. No matter which way I turned, I could not get comfortable. I am sure I kept Denise up most of the night. The next day it was obvious something was wrong with me.

I woke up feeling nauseated; I couldn't keep any thing down. I tried to eat a little breakfast, but in no time at all, everything I ate came right up. Once I started vomiting, I knew I was going to be in for a long ride. I had no idea how bumpy the road was about to get.

I have experienced this feeling a few times since the kidney transplant. I tried to brace myself, and wait for it to pass. On the other hand, every time things started this way, it was a clear sign it wasn't going to get any better.

Denise always tried to get me to go to the hospital when the symptoms started. She didn't like for me to wait until things got out of control, but I was little bit on the stubborn side. I always thought I could handle it. I don't know why I would take that route because it never worked. Based on my previous experiences, these were all signs I was going to end up in the hospital, regardless. It didn't bother me; I was always a natural born fighter anyway. I never felt right throwing my hands up at the sight of trouble. I like to feel I have at least stepped in the ring for the fight.

After a while, it became evident I should have listened to Denise, but I didn't. Long story short, I got sicker than I had been in a long time. Denise had to call the paramedics to come and get me. They rushed me to the hospital. My symptoms were not very distinctive. At first, they thought I had a touch of food poisoning since this started after I had eaten fast food. The doctors ran several tests. All the tests revealed there wasn't anything wrong with the food I had eaten. The food just didn't agree with my system. All the grease was too much for my body to process at one time.

Since I had undergone the transplant surgery, my immune system was way out of whack. Foods I could process before didn't seem to agree with me now. The doctors wanted to make sure they had everything under control, so they kept me in the hospital for about four days. As a kidney transplant patient, this wasn't too unusual. What was unusual was my follow up treatment. It was recommended I have four steroid treatments within the next week. It would help to flush out my kidneys. This didn't seem like too big of a deal to me. I would periodically go to the Dallas Transplant Institute (DTI), to have them check on my kidneys.

All the treatments were set up on an outpatient basis. The treatments were to be done on four consecutive days with about five hundred milligrams of steroids taken intravenously each day. Before I began the treatments, the doctor explained the possible side effects from the steroids. Looking down on his notepad, the doctor said, *"You could experience some back pain, high blood sugar, anxiety and even a bit of anxiousness."*

As we listened to him, Denise and I looked at each other and nodded our heads in agreement. None of these symptoms seemed like something I could not handle. I felt the worst part was over; I was just ready to get back home where things would be normal, at least the normal I had grown to know over the last few years.

Before we left the hospital, a nurse went over the possible side effects with us again. She said, *"If any of these symptoms transpire, please let us know. We can work with you as we go forward with your treatments."* Reaching for the door to the office, I smiled at her because I knew I was going to be fine. I just responded, *"Okay."* Denise and I didn't talk much on the way home. We both assumed this was just a snag in the road. Everything was getting ready to be back on track.

Before I went to work on Tuesday morning, I started the steroid treatments. It only took about ten minutes for the first treatment. I went to work, came home and rested. It was a good day. The next day, I had the second treatment; I was still doing fine. I did not have any of the side effects they mentioned at the hospital.

On Thursday morning I had the third treatment. After that treatment, I started feeling a tinge of back pain. I was also beginning to feel somewhat anxious. This still was not enough to alarm me. It didn't even bother Denise because I only had one more treatment. We both knew my tolerance level for medication was very high because of my past drug addiction.

Friday morning, the end of my work-week and all things were well. I had my last and final treatment before I headed to work that day. Sunday I went to church, but during service I started to feel a little different. All of a sudden a weird feeling came over my entire body. I couldn't quite put my finger on it, but something was different. I came home and got some rest. By that night, I began to feel a little funky, to say the least.

Monday morning, I got out of bed a little slow and disoriented. I was still determined not to let this get the best of me. I got up and somehow managed to make it through the day. On Tuesday morning, I had to admit I was done.

I was dealing with every side effect the doctors mentioned to me at first. My anxiety level was at an all-time high. I was so anxious I could not even keep still. I had never experienced anything like this, not even when I was doing drugs to get high. It was such a weird and uncomfortable feeling it scared me. I felt completely out of control.

Denise was baffled by my condition. She knew something was wrong, but she could not pinpoint it. Finally, she asked me, *"Baby, what do you want to do?"* All I could say was, *"I don't know what to do."*

I didn't know if I wanted to sit up; I didn't know if I wanted to lay down. I didn't even know if I wanted to walk around the house. One minute I was in a chair, the next minute I was standing up. Then I would start walking around with no destination in mind. Denise started referring to me as Mad Max. I was over the edge. I knew she couldn't figure out what to do with me because I couldn't calm down.

It's funny how God orchestrates things. The only reason Denise was home in the first place was because her alternator had gone out in her car. Normally she would have been at work. I needed her now like I never needed her before. I didn't know what was going on, but something was drastically wrong.

After observing my erratic behavior, Denise grabbed her purse and said, *"Baby, we have got to go."* We headed to the emergency room. I have been there many times before, but this was going to be a time I would never forget. When we arrived at the hospital, I felt like I was going to lose it.

I walked in and sat down while Denise signed me in. I was still out of it; I did not feel like myself at all. It was as if I was having an out of body experience. I was there, but I wasn't there. I felt like I was going crazy. As I sat in the waiting room, I felt a little heat surge go through my body. I wanted to pass out just to eliminate all these weird feelings that were going on in my body.

It was awkward. I knew I was at the hospital to be treated, but I still didn't want to be bothered. I got up just like I was going to walk out the door. Then Denise said, *"Where are you going?"* Not knowing what was going on, I responded, *"I don't know."*

She managed to get me back in my seat, but I couldn't sit still. I just slumped down in the chair. As I slipped down in the seat, Denise yelled, *"Oh, no you don't."* She knew if I passed out, trying to move my body was going to be almost impossible. She also knew if I ever really let go, it was going to be hard to get me back. She wanted to make sure I stayed conscious and alert as possible until they could get me in to see the doctor. There was no doubt she had a challenge on her hands.

Like always, Denise was the woman for the job. We had been through so much since I had my kidney transplant. There was no way we could have known this incident would be a major setback for us. This would shake the very foundation of our world.

H.G.

As I continued to go through all these crazy antics in the waiting room, Denise was on watch. When I started to walk around, she would make me sit down. When I would try to wiggle out of my seat, she made me sit up. She started rubbing my back to ease the pain and calm me down. In the midst of the chaos, her touch was reassuring. I don't even know if I would have made it if she weren't there. When I say "guardian angel", that is who she was and still is to me.

I know it could not have taken that long to be admitted, but it seemed like forever. The longer they took, the weirder I started acting. All of a sudden it would feel like I needed to go to the bathroom. So I would jump up and start walking. Then Denise would ask, "*Where are you going?*"
In my bewildered state, all I could say is, "*I don't know.*"

Before I could get too far, she was right there grabbing my hand leading me back to my seat in the waiting room. This had to be the weirdest feeling I have ever had in my life. I began to wonder to myself, am I going crazy? There was no way I could begin to understand or make any sense of what was happening to me. The only hope I had, that made sense, was the fact that I had just taken two thousand milligrams of steroids in the last week. I knew that somehow the treatments had to be the blame for my reaction. This was the only thing different from my normal routine.

Once they admitted me, they began to run tests. It was evident my body could not handle the steroid treatments. My creatine levels sky-rocketed to about a level five. The creatine level tells how well the kidneys are operating. My normal baseline level, as the recipient of a transplant, is about two. The average person may have a level of point fifteen, to about a one point two.   At one point, my creatine levels elevated to about a seven, more than triple what my normal level is.

Originally, the high steroids were being used to flush out any blockage in my kidneys. Since it didn't work, I had to have another procedure to place a stent in my kidneys. There were some complications with the process, which caused one of my kidneys to be bruised. This put me in an indefinite holding pattern. My patience was wearing thin. My few days' hospital visit turned into a few weeks. I felt like my back was against the ropes. This was worst than my initial transplant. When I first had the transplant, I knew what to expect. This time I was living out the unexpected.

In desperation I sent out an SOS to Bishop Jakes. My emotions were all over the place. I was totally out of control. There was no way I could make it through this situation by myself. I needed help. I know the Word of God says, "*The prayers of the righteous availeth much*," and I knew I needed much prayer.

I realized I was in trouble. I reached out to Bishop's Executive Assistant, Beverly. I asked her to get word to Bishop that I needed the church to pray for me. She sent a text message to Bishop Saturday night. I heard when he got the text, he said, "*Oh no, I have got to go see Holloway!*"

Bishop knew me. He knew as private as I am, for me to ask the church to pray for me, meant I had to be in dire straits.

Bishop interpreted the text message as my distress signal, and he was right.

I lay in bed wondering what in the world was going to happen next. Before my mind could wander too far, I heard a knock at my hospital room door. In my weak and scratchy voice I said, "Come in." I knew that it had to be an orderly wanting to take more blood, or a nurse wanting to take my temperature.
To my surprise, towering at the door was Bishop Jakes, my friend, my pastor, and my boss. He had come to see about me. I laid there helpless, but seeing him reminded me that I did have hope.

I was so weak and frustrated. I had been pushing the doctors for answers all week long, but I had not gotten any. I was irritated and aggravated. I wanted some answers; it didn't even have to be the right answers. All the doctors seemed to be so slothful; they weren't coming up with any solution or resolution.

Bishop already knew the gist of the problem. Without saying much, he came and sat in the chair by my hospital bed. I began to share with him all the details of what was going on. I told him, "*I asked the doctors what the final result would be. I just want them to give me the worst case scenario. They said that I could lose one of the kidneys, and that I could possibly go back on dialysis. I think that I can deal with that.*"

I looked at Bishop's face as he digested the information that I had had just given him. I could not wait for his response. He just leaned toward me and said, "*Holloway, I know you. Don't push these doctors.*" He paused and added, "*I know that you are frustrated, aggravated, and I know that you are angry. If you push these doctors they are going to make a decision that you might regret later on.*"

As I listened to him, a spirit of peace came over me. I hadn't been thinking about the situation like that. I just wanted an answer...*now*.

Looking me straight in the eyes, Bishop said, *"You are thinking about where you are right now. But the reality is that you need to think about when you are in your 70s or 80s. Don't allow them to take a kidney if it is not necessary. Wait it out. Slow down. Take your time. Holloway, use this experience to learn patience."*

He paused and added, *"Whatever you need ...we got you. You need a DVD; we are going to get it for you. You need a CD, we going to get it. You need tapes; we are going to get it. Whatever you need, we got you. Holloway, just slow your tail down."*

After we had talked for a while, Bishop's parting words were, *"You can't make a rash decision right now. You have to think about your later years. You are still a young man, and you don't realize that because of the situation you are in."*
He prayed with me. Then he and his friends loved on me. As he was walking out the door, he looked back at me one last time and said, *"Take your time, and you will be fine."*

Before I knew it, just as quickly as he had entered the room, he was gone. His visit was like a breath of fresh air for me. My countenance had changed and my spirit had been lifted. God was setting me up for my healing. Bishop had caught me at a down moment, but his words had brought me back up again. There was so much wisdom in what he said to me. It was encouraging, to know that God had used the Man of God to deliver a rhema word to me in a time of crisis.

That night, I had heard God's voice through Bishop Jakes. It was amazing. That night I began to calm down. I started to release the anxiousness that held me hostage over the last few weeks.

After Bishop left, I reflected on a prayer that I had received from Bishop Duncan-Williams after I had my kidney transplant. Bishop Duncan-Williams was from Ghana. He had prophesied over me and told me that there was a lineage that had been passed on through my blood-line that needed to be broken. Once I found that out, I told myself that I was going to stand up to it and break the lineage. I didn't want this curse to go through another generation.

Over the next few days, I slowed down and began to focus on being healed. My doctors had finished visiting with me. I was sitting in the chair in my room with the door open. I kept seeing these two men dressed in black walking past the door. It really didn't faze me as long as they were just passing by my door. But when they stopped at my door, it agitated me. I really didn't want to be bothered. I had been pinched, poked and pricked. I had nurses, doctors and interns in my room like clockwork, all times of the day. I didn't need the presence of another strange face in my room.

My displeasure in their appearance didn't seem to affect them in the least. They proceeded to enter my room and introduce themselves to me as chaplains. As far as I was concerned, their presence was not welcomed. First of all, I didn't know them. Secondly, I wasn't feeling the best. I knew that this was not going to be a good visit. Extending their hands, one of the gentlemen said, "We would just like to pray with you."

When they said "prayer," my heart melted. I knew that prayer was the answer. I perked up and said, "Let's do it then."

As I extended my hands, one of the gentlemen started leading the prayer. I could not believe it; something in me began to leap as the prayers went forth. I had been crying out to God asking him *"When, when, when?"* When I heard the prayers going forth, it was like all at once I could hear the heavens opening up. I got my answer once again. It was almost like my experience of getting free from drugs in my bathtub. The answer was, *"Now!"*

I didn't know these guys from Adam, but their prayers had given me a release. They gave me the confirmation that I needed that things were about to turn around. Once they finished praying, I felt complete.

After they left the room, I was so shaken up that I could not stop weeping. It took me about 30 minutes to pull myself together. There was only one time that I remember a prayer that was that powerful. It was the prayer of Bishop Duncan-Williams several years ago.

When Bishop Duncan-Williams prayed with me, he prayed as though he was bringing heaven to me. These same guys prayed exactly like he had prayed for me. I wondered if these guys were from Ghana. As I was looking toward the door, I noticed them walking down the hallway again. I called out for them to come back. When they came in the room, I asked the guys for their business cards. While one of them was reaching in his pocket. I asked him, *"Where ya'll from?"* With a very distinct accent one of the gentlemen said, *"We are from Ghana."*

I threw my head back in my chair and let out a big, *"Whooo!"* It blew me away. God was definitely up to something, because there was a connection between these guys that were strangers and Bishop Duncan-Williams. God was connecting the dots over the last eight years, the way that Bishop Duncan-Williams had prayed and the way these guys had prayed for me. Do I have a revelation on what this meant? No, I don't. But I got a connection from it.

With that being said, I formed a friendship with these guys. When we finished, they prayed over me again. When they left my room, a spirit of laugher overtook me. I knew then that it had been settled in the heavens. The lineage had been broken. The process was settled. I no longer had to worry about when this ordeal was going to be over. For me the greatest part was already over.

God had taught me a very valuable lesson through an illness that I didn't even understand. I had to learn to **trust God when I could not trace Him**. He had broken everything in me to make sure that my steps were ordered by Him. I was no longer walking in the shadows; I was stepping into His marvelous light. This time there were no blinders on my eyes. The Word of God was giving me sight, and I was about to see life in a new way. It was almost like the song, *Amazing Grace*. I once was blind, but now I see.

* Scripture Reference

"But without faith it is impossible to please Him: for he that cometh to God must believe that He is, and that He is a rewarder of them that diligently seek Him."

Hebrews 11:6 (KJV)

* Prayer

Lord, not my will but Thy will be done. Allow me to stop wondering what is next and rest in the fact my next step is coming from You: the Author and Finisher of my faith.

H.G.

CHAPTER SIXTEEN

Covered By The Blood: Last Steps Of The Journey

"But if we walk in the light, as He is in the light, we have fellowship one with another, and the blood of Jesus Christ His Son cleanseth us from all sin."

~1 John 1:7

I thought that once I got out of the hospital my biggest health hurdle would be over. Little did I know that I was about to face something that would make my long hospital visit seem like a cakewalk. I was only out of the hospital for a few weeks when I started feeling very sick. I had diarrhea. I was throwing up, and my creatine levels went through the roof. My creatine levels were higher than they had ever been. This was a sign that my kidneys were not functioning properly. This was almost like I had taken a step backward to the point before I had the kidney transplant.

When we let my doctor know what was going on, he did not hesitate to tell me to report to the hospital. This time when I entered the hospital, I had no idea what to expect. I had just been hospitalized for over a month. It seemed that I had dealt with everything that I could have imagined. All I could think was: *now what?*

I still had stents in each of my kidneys. They were being used to help eliminate any blockage between my kidney and my bladder. The doctors decided to remove the stents because of the problems that I was having. The next thing that happened was almost unthinkable. They determined that the pediatric kidneys, which I had gotten over 8 years prior, had become infected. This could be very serious for me, so they had to remove my kidneys. It was clear that I would have to do dialysis again.

I had been anxious during my last hospitalization. Yet, this time I had a different outlook. Now, I was facing the worst possible scenario, and I wasn't blinking an eye. I wasn't counting how many days this was going to take. I didn't even ask when I was going to be able to leave. I didn't wonder what would be next. I guess God was preparing me for the fact that I would not be able to handle what was next.

It was at this moment that I realized Bishop Jakes' request had been answered. He had suggested that I use this experience to learn patience. It is amazing how patience will rest on your shoulders when you run out of other options. I had nothing to do, but to wait for God to move. For the first time in my life, I had no answers and I was okay with that. My surgeries were coming so close together that I could no longer keep up with them. My body felt like a puppet. I was being poked, and prodded every few minutes.

With only a few days between operations, my body did not have time to recover from the pain. After they removed my kidneys, my abdomen became bloated. The bloating was a sign to the doctors that something else was wrong. Then I had another emergency surgery to find the source of the problem. During my third operation, they discovered, I had an infection in my blood stream. After this exploratory operation, fluid built up in my lungs and I also developed bacterial pneumonia.

The exploratory operation would be the last thing that I would remember for a while. After that operation, time stood still for me. For the next nine days, my body teetered between life and death, like a man walking a tight rope in the circus. Any slight movement to the left or to the right could have been fatal. I spent nine consecutive days in the Intensive Care Unit of Methodist Hospital.

My memory during this time period is almost nonexistent. I had to rely on Denise's details for what happened. For the most part, I was in a medically induced coma. Some people said I responded to them when they came to visit. I know that it had to be on a subconscious level because I don't remember much of anything. I do remember Denise and Bishop Jakes visiting me.

There is one thing about life: you never really know what is going to be up the road. Once you decide what direction you are going in, there is bound to be a curve down the way. Being in ICU was a major curve in my journey. Denise, who has always been my first line of defense, became my gate-keeper. She was the only one who received all the information about my treatment, my options and my condition. I can only imagine what this had to be like for her. She was faced with having someone that she loved be completely helpless.

My condition forced her to switch gears as a caretaker. She had already started documenting all my various medications, the possible side effects and every date and time that a procedure was done. Now she also had to keep up with doctors and their directives.

For almost two weeks, Denise was my guardian angel. She kept guard over my very life, as my existence dangled in the face of death. She had to pray, be patient and protect her heart from all the information that was being tossed her way by the medical team at the hospital.

The cardiologist and the pulmonologist were seeing me several times a day because they were monitoring my heart and lungs. They did daily chest and lung x-rays to monitor any significant change.

During this time, Dr. Jose Castillo-Lugo MD, who was my nephrologist, spoke to Denise. He had been with me since my initial kidney transplant. He told her that I was a very sick man. These words were piecing to her spirit. With all that I had been through, she had never heard these words before.

Denise is a very strong woman. She knew that this situation was not for someone that was easily shaken. There was no doubt that this was going to be a fight. She rolled up her sleeves and jumped in the ring swinging. Instead of the doctor's words scaring her, they propelled her to prayer. She began to pray about everything. She prayed about what was going on and what was needed to resolve it. As my condition advanced from serious to critical, Denise tried to remain calm.

She was very calculated in who came around me and the words that were spoken over me. She didn't want any one around me that did not believe that I was going to make it through this situation.

Of course, people at all four of The Potter's House locations were praying. Our faith also became contagious at the hospital. Even one of the head nurses began to impart words of encouragement to Denise about my situation. She shared with her how she had seen other patients pull through similar circumstances.

As she waited by my side, Denise was constantly making confessions about our Lord and Savior Jesus Christ. Although the situation looked bleak, she knew that my strength did not rest in men; it rested in the Lord. Of course, I needed the doctors to do what they do. But, when they had exhausted their efforts we both knew that God had the final say-so. With everything that was in her, Denise held on to the fact that the Lord was my master physician.

While I was in intensive care, every day was a challenge. My temperature fluctuated between 102 and 105. When it reached 105, they placed ice packs under my armpits and around my neck to bring it down. Then, my temperature dropped to 95 degrees. My low body temperature was just as critical as when it was high. When the body temperature drops below 95 degrees, hypothermia sets in. Hypothermia usually happens before someone freezes to death. It will cause the body organs to shut down. Since my low body temperature could be fatal, they had to bring in a vacuum type device. It was placed around me like a warm blanket to help re-warm my body and elevate my body temperature.

A breathing tube also had to be placed in my mouth because my oxygen level was so low. I had about 5 other tubes in me at the same time. The doctors knew that they had to get rid of the infection in my blood stream. They explained to Denise that the only solution was to do dialysis for 24 hours. Yet, they didn't have any idea of how long they were going to have to continue in order to clear up the infection.

Even as strong as Denise is, I think that she started to get a little squeamish at the idea of me receiving dialysis nonstop for 24 hours. This is about the time that Bishop Jakes came in to see me again. I wasn't breathing on my own, I was on continuous dialysis, and the infection in my blood was not clearing up. The hope of my surviving this was fading with every passing moment.

On day five of my stay in Intensive Care, Bishop Jakes posted a 911 message on the Potter's House Facebook page. He requested that the saints bombard heaven with prayers for me. He knew that my survival was contingent on prayers being as aggressive as my treatment was. His Facebook post was received with great enthusiasm. People around the country were posting and reposting. Then they began to tweet the request as well. Some people knew me, others didn't, but everybody was praying. Before long, there were thousands of prayers that began to go forth from across the country. There were prayers, prayers and more prayers as Bishop's prayer request became viral.

The next day, I was started on a feeding tube. I had gone several days without any form of nutrition. By this time, Denise was adamant about who came to see me. According to her, *"my condition was not for the faint of heart."* My immune system was also very weak, and it would have been easy for me to catch an infection from someone that had just stopped by to pay their well wishes.

No matter how bad things got, Denise would not leave my side. The worst things were, the more diligent she became. Gritting her teeth, she was standing on the word of God. She did not flinch, as she held on to what God had placed in her spirit. Deep in her spirit, she knew that this was not my time to go. She was not afraid of what the devil might try to make her think. It was only God's word that she held before her as she was given various reports from the doctors.

Once Denise thought things might be okay. She then got another piece of shocking news. The doctors could not regulate my heart rate. My heart was beating very erratically. It became the cardiologist's job to come up with a resolution to the new impending problem with my heart.

After evaluating the situation, he came in and spoke to Denise. He said, "I am going to have to flip your husband's heart." His words were more than Denise could comprehend. "What do you mean, you are going to have to flip his heart?" she inquired.

The doctor explained that my blood pressure was low and my heart rate was up. This meant that my heart was working too hard to keep my body going. I could not last long like this. The basic rhythm of my heart was off. The only option that they had, to get things back in sync was to stop my heart and restart it again.

As Denise began to digest this new piece of information, the doctor said, "I don't want to overwhelm you, but we will have to bring in a defibrillator. This is just a precaution, in case his heart does not restart on its own."

Then the doctors had Denise sign a waiver so that they could proceed with the procedure.

I am sure that Denise's hands had to be shaking as she signed the piece of paper. Then she walked out into the waiting room. The doctor said, "I will come and get you in about 15 minutes."

Almost emotionless, she waited for the doctor to come out into the waiting room. Like clockwork, 15 minutes later. The doctors came in to get Denise.

With a smile on his face he said, *"It was successful."*

On day eight, the doctors slowly began to bring me out of sedation. After being in a coma for almost a week, I was finally starting to stabilize. By day nine, I had reached a turning point. I was released from ICU to return to a regular room. Coming to myself made me appreciate life even more. Even though I didn't know what was going on, my spirit would not give up. Deep in my soul, I knew that God still had a greater work for me to do.

In all my life, I had never come this close to dying. It was like my nose was right up against the doorway to death. I was starring death in the face, but I still could not cross over. Getting into a normal room was a huge sign to me that my life was getting back on track. The first time I laid my eyes on Denise, it was like looking at an angel. All the time I was in ICU, I could feel her presence. Now, I could actually see her face again.

As I began to get my strength back, Denise went over everything that had happened to me in great detail. Based on everything that she shared with me, it was evident that the doctors had done everything that they could to preserve my life. Yet, still I knew that God had shown his hand. There was no doubt in my mind that my survival was simply a miracle. As I reflect over my situation, I thought about all the people that I had heard who passed this year. My eyes started to water up,

I could not believe that God thought enough of me to keep me on this road a little while longer. I was grateful.

Even when God's hand moves in your favor, things can be challenging. My biggest surprise came the first time I tried to stand up. Then, I realized something was wrong. When I could not stand on my own, I asked someone to help me up to my feet. Yet, even though I was standing, I could not get my legs to work. I was devastated. I had no idea what was going on. My head dropped down to my chest. Then I realized that I had forgotten how to walk.

My voice was raspy from having the tube that was down my throat. Nothing was like I thought it would be. I was still alive, but now I was going to have to take baby steps to get back on my journey to health.

You never realize how fragile life is until you are faced with death. My entire prospective changed during this last experience. I know that my journey has not always been smooth, but now I know that God still has a much greater work for me to do.

Over the last decade, God has been setting me up to break a generational curse in my family. I still remember Archbishop Duncan-Williams telling me that the issue with my family was going to stop with me. I should have known then that this was not going to be an easy process.

My last health challenge could have easily been the end, but it wasn't. It was the beginning. I went through several weeks of rehabilitation so that I could regain my strength. In no time, I was able to walk again.

Finally, I was able to return home. I still have to continue dialysis three times a week. Each session is about 4 hours. This means my dialysis treatments are almost like a part-time job.

Once again, I am waiting for a kidney. But, I am in no way discouraged. In fact, I am encouraged. I know that God is not through with me yet. As my life hung in the balance, my existence was dependent on my blood being purified. For a while, that seemed impossible. The Bible tells us in Mark 9: 23 (KJV), *"If thou canst believe, all things are possible to him that believeth."*

I am now a living witness of what I learned as a little boy in Sunday school. There is nothing like the Blood of Jesus. As Christians, we know that the Blood of Jesus can wash away our sins. His blood washed away my childhood antics, my drug addiction, and the various issues that I have dealt with in my life.

When my blood became infected, I believe God replaced it with His blood. Now my commission is even greater. I have no idea when my journey will end, but until it does I will continue to walk in the shadow of greatness. With the light of the Lord behind me, I will boldly step towards whatever he has next for me.

* Scripture Reference

"May you have loving-favor and peace from Jesus Christ Who is faithful in telling the truth. Jesus Christ is the first to be raised from the dead. He is the head over all the kings of the earth. He is the One Who loves us and has set us free from our sins by His blood."

Revelation 1:5 (KJV)

* Prayer

Lord, I don't know where this journey is going to take me. Yet, I know with You all things are possible. I no longer even have a fear of death, because I am covered by Your blood.

H.G.

HOLLOWAY GRAY

"Despise not the small beginning"

Holloway Gray holds over 25 years of experience in servant-hood, which began with volunteering before becoming full-time ministry.

Mr. Gray began his call to ministry as a volunteer in 1989 after joining the church under Bishop Jakes' leadership. He volunteered in audio duplication; helping to package, ship and sell product. He assisted with conference details and greeting delegates at the meetings.

He was consecrated as a Deacon in 1993. Two years later he began traveling and serving, both as a Deacon to the church and armor bearer to Bishop Jakes.

Mr. Gray has trained other Deacons and men in the church to serve as armor-bearers and security protection. He has mentored a volunteer base of deacons who rotated under his leadership, in serving Bishop Jakes. He has shared his teaching and training on various occasions both in workshop and individual training sessions.

Holloway served as Executive Coordinator to Bishop Jakes for over ten years. This entailed management of the Executive Offices' business details, and specifically Bishop Jakes travel itinerate.

His current role is Campus Administrator at The Potter's House of Fort Worth, where he oversees the day-to-day operations of the ministry under the pastorate of Pastor Patrick Winfield.

He and his wife, Denise, have been married for thirty-two years and reside in the suburbs of Dallas, TX.

H.G.

H.G.

CPSIA information can be obtained at www.ICGtesting.com
Printed in the USA
BVOW09s1218221214

380423BV00024B/322/P